Beyond
THE
SUNSET

Beyond THE SUNSET

Samantha Noelle

Beyond Borders
Publishing
SAMANTHA NOELLE

BEYOND THE SUNSET

Published by
Beyond Borders Publishing
www.beyondborderspublishing.com
For more information or to request permissions: beyondborderspublishing@gmail.com

ISBN (paperback): 978-1-66786-787-8
ISBN (EPUB): 978-1-66786-788-5

Registered at the United States Copyright Office
First paperback edition: September 2022

Cover & Interior Design: BookBaby
Line Edit & Developmental Evaluation: Ann Castro, Ann Castro Studio
Proofreaders: Adana Gardner Marfield & Randen Gardner

To my dear friend and angel, Jane.

You are the light that carried me through
the telling of your story.

As an author, I discovered my soul purpose and
overcame my fears to reach for the stars.

Your one wish was that your story would change lives—
and it has changed mine profoundly.

I am forever grateful.

"I can still remember watching those vibrant sunsets, sitting close to my mother and baby boy. We'd find refuge on those rolling hillsides and within our wakeful silence, the serenity lay between us. God had carried us home."

—JANE CORSARO

A Word From Jane

I was eighty-three when I began my confession—the story of my life. Raw, unscripted, truthful. It's a story I share in hopes that it will provide another surviving heart some comfort and shed some light. Because through struggles, we endure, and grace provides mercy.

Let me start by asking a simple question. What has been the purpose of your life? Take a few seconds to reflect, and then ask yourself this: Are my eyes mainly open or mostly shut?

Some of us walk with our eyes closed even when we're awake. As a result, we often take things for granted, like the fact that we can see, taste, and smell. Skipping over the chapters in our daily routines, we can forget the treasures that lie in front of us or the monsters at our back. There's a reason for everything that coexists in our lives—and we all play a part in history, surrounded by an infinite universe. We all have a story to tell. Whether it's primarily light or dark is not the question, but rather, are you living your life honestly?

The truth is this: My emotions have been buried till this point. I, the forgotten child of the 1930s, have finally triumphed and moved closer to an awakening spirit, equipped with the understanding that my final hours are drawing near.

There was a time when I dreamed of becoming an actress in Hollywood, but instead, I was an actress on the world's stage, perhaps the greatest place a woman like me could be. I played every role life dished out with tact and intelligence, choosing to fight for my life rather than end it because I knew God's plan was greater than my own.

This is why, even now, after surviving the shame and neglect I faced in my youth and beyond, my faith is still secure in God.

As I neared eighty, it became clear to some that I couldn't live alone any longer. At that age, your mind wants to keep up, but your body is just too tired. My son realized I needed more care when he received a phone call that I was malnourished and in the hospital. In an effort to save myself, I agreed to move closer to him. I left my little red house in McKeesport, Pennsylvania for an assisted living community across the United States. Internally it felt like a death wish, leaving my belongings behind, but somewhere in the glimmer of the horizon, it dawned on me that there was more for me to live for.

Leaving McKeesport felt like a punishment at first, a cruel reminder that we all have an expiration date and a time when we need to decide who will take care of us. It took the warrior in me to leave my home after the estate sale. It was a final goodbye to a dear friend because my home anchored me to the past, something I knew I would never return to.

On the final day, as I started to pull the door shut, a wind pushed against it like an army of soldiers at war with my heart. My knees buckled. I dug my heels into the porch's wooden planks for one last thrust. The bitter wind at my back sailed overhead as I smelled the scent of age exchange a final farewell. Faintly, I tugged once again, catching my breath.

It shut, it shut, it shut. Those words coursed through my veins and replayed every moment, every story, and every emotion that had been shed inside those walls. That's what no one realizes about giving up your independence. You're not a child just because you lose traction; you're an adult in a body being taken over by gravity.

There, in the gray winter of Pennsylvania, that long chapter of my life had finally ended.

After what seemed like a dream, my plane landed in Las Vegas on March 17, 2017. I reluctantly entered the assisted living facility's Glory Room and set down my suitcase at my heels. When I lifted my head, I was struck by the room's beautiful structure. It was an empress. Her ethereal castle-like walls towered above me, casting a glow of golden light. The opulent indoor waterfall cascaded down the sides of a grand fireplace. It felt heavenly, and it overwhelmed my tarnished spirit.

The Glory Room nurtured me with its quiet touch of classical music as I, in deep thought, ran my fingers along the fine silk curtains. I could smell the fresh spray of flowers lining the mantels and hear the wind chimes blowing in the distant courtyard gardens. Never in my wildest dreams would I have imagined that this place would open my heart to new beginnings. We may have been the elderly ones who could no longer care for ourselves, but we also were the vessels holding stories that were more powerful than legends.

The Glory Room resurrected me from the cocoon I had placed myself in. Never had I imagined my story being brought to life.

Eventually, after I had settled in, an earth angel found me. A woman's silhouette approached, and an instant soul-connection ignited. She rescued me in my raw gardens of heaven and hell and offered to help me release the manuscript that had been living within me—the story I'd carried for eighty-three years. Under her spotlight, my youth felt reborn.

Samantha was her name. And we spent the next few years meeting in her office, building a friendship as we painted the portrait of my life.

Each of us sheds a story like a snake sheds its skin. I hope my story will influence and inspire you. Life is a gift. Embrace it.

Author Preface

As Jane's writer, I've learned how powerful the human spirit is and that the only thing we truly need is love because we have nothing but our memories in the end. You never see a U-Haul following a hearse.

Jane gave me my confidence back and inspired me to write. Her wisdom, honesty, and strength united us. We were in sync like two sailors in a windstorm about to embark on the greatest journey of our lives.

I saw the world differently through her eyes and adored her bravery, passion, and perseverance. It helped me trust the process of listening and crafting her story.

The Glory Room

There was a special place in the assisted living facility where I worked. I named it the Glory Room because it had become the light away from the darkness outside our windowpanes: disturbing posts on social media, gun violence, drugs, and war. Inside its safe walls, the Glory Room celebrated our residents—strong-willed men and magnificent women— whose lives and inspiring stories touched and blessed me.

They were loyal to Frank Sinatra, talked about man's greatest achievements, saluted our war heroes, and believed in the American dream, a foundation our forefathers had built that was being eroded outside our sanctuary.

The Glory Room held endless tracks of memories and life lessons. For those of us who paid attention, we learned the importance of our tomorrows and that material possessions mean nothing when our final hours approach. But I wondered, what will we say in those hours? Who will be there to listen?

It was easy in that special room to forget that time exists. The days ran into one another while we sang our favorite songs and built traditions. We were a family, the only family that some residents had. At times, we were the only spark that ignited their will to live, and we were the hands that held theirs during their last breath.

Meeting Jane

Jane was an ageless firecracker—with defined cheekbones, pale-green eyes, and short, white, feathered hair—who held herself high with dignity and never asked for much. She kept to her routine, taking brisk walks every morning up and down the hallways like a freight train searching for salvation. She was an attractive lady whose spirit danced with youthfulness as she'd move her hips in stride to the music. Her personality was electrifying, and the Glory Room always went wild watching her vanish inside the rhythm during our monthly parties. I admired her from afar and learned from her that life was just that … a dance.

Jane had many talents and was a wonderful actress. During our Actors Theater program, she executed every role as if she'd already lived it. And behind the lens, she was a determined woman ready to speak. Her deteriorating health gave her the courage to come forward. The curtain was closing, but she had the last word.

After a few months in the Glory Room, Jane and I became the best of friends as she shared parts of her life one moment to the next.

It was then that I felt called to complete her journey and committed to writing her story.

We started the rough draft in my small office located on the third floor. When you looked out to the west, there were picturesque views of the Red Rock Mountains. Early in the mornings, I'd open the blinds and gaze out at the sunrise, a light that would bring Jane and me together. I called it divine providence because something unexpected was at play. That's the thing about life. It's unpredictable.

At times, her words clung to me—a faint outcry of glory tucked under her pain. A pain that must have felt a million miles high. But I, too, had felt her heaviness on those days when it was difficult to hold back the tears. Her survival instincts inspired me, and her life was a mixed canvas of beauty and tragedy.

Lying in bed one evening, after writing for a few hours, I wondered if we were somehow the same person reincarnated. We were knitted together by an internal search for God, various types of crises, the entrapment of abuse and seclusion, and the heart's endurance to be broken and unbroken.

The nature in which we perceive life is born of many firestorms that shape who we are.

It was important for her to leave behind her legacy as a testament of faith. As Jane's writer, I was moved. Her story awakened me. Was the emptiness in my life the proverbial elephant in the room, a harbinger of healing hovering over my breaking point that Jane had revived? Everyone I knew saw me as an illumination of hope and happiness. However, behind the fairytale façade, lived the other me: the stepmother, the wife, and, sometimes, the witch riddled with resentment, yearning for control.

Jane helped me find peace. It was her story that unchained me from my chaos and birthed my new life.

Contents

A Word From Jane i

Author Preface v

Chapter 1 Remnant Confessions - A Story Is Born 1

Chapter 2 Slim Pickings 13

Chapter 3 A Little Piece of Heaven - A Whole Lot of Hell 20

Chapter 4 Spiritual Darkness 27

Chapter 5 Growing Pains 42

Chapter 6 War Time in America 50

Chapter 7 Puppets on a String 57

Chapter 8 Hearts of Men - Part 1 68

Chapter 9 Hearts of Men - Part 2 77

Chapter 10 Trash in a Silk Suit 90

Chapter 11 The Beasts of the River 94

Chapter 12 The Gapa Club 103

Chapter 13 Sugar and Spice 110

Chapter 14 Sloppy Seconds 117

Chapter 15 Alfie 126

Chapter 16 A Witch at My Door 139

Chapter 17 Evil Walks In..148

Chapter 18 Battleships and Broomsticks..................................156

Chapter 19 Deadly Nightshade..163

Chapter 20 Uncle Thurman and The Holy Spirit.........................175

Chapter 21 Message from Above..184

Chapter 22 A King in Turmoil..193

Chapter 23 Life After Death...203

Chapter 24 Uninvited..208

Chapter 25 A Walk in the Clouds..213

Chapter 26 Baby Blues...220

Chapter 27 Chariot of Truth..226

Chapter 28 Beyond the Sunset...229

Epilogue From the Author...232

About Samantha Noelle...235

Chapter 1

REMNANT CONFESSIONS -
A STORY IS BORN

When you live in the dark, you become exposed to internal monsters, the ones that can claim a life, slay a family, or throw your soul into the pits of hell. Nothing is ever promised. Take my eyesight, for example. After contracting a blood vessel disease, I have had no guarantee that I'll be able to see the light tomorrow, but I am certain the darkness will never fade.

There is no reversal for my vision loss. I can't repair the damage with a magic wand, nor smooth the wrinkles of my life story.

Early Years: Glassport, PA
1930s

I was born Jane Louise Quinn in Glassport, Pennsylvania on September 22, 1935, to my parents, Cora Quinn and Martin Quinn, whom everyone called Fish.

My mother was an attractive woman with long hair, deep-set eyes, and a shapely body. She always looked her best and never left the house without lipstick and a pack of cigarettes. Calm and collected, she refrained from smiling too much because of two crooked front teeth that made her uniquely beautiful but trumped her confidence.

Despite that, she was a master at making men swoon—although she never realized it—and a bona fide narcissist. For those sporadic times when she was endearing to me, she was Mum. But much of the time, I thought of her as Cora.

My father bore a striking resemblance to the actor Steve McQueen. His jet-black hair, rough shave, and mysteriously attractive emerald eyes caught people's attention. Even with his ruddy complexion and a few missing teeth, he was handsome.

And I never underestimated him. Father was a well-built machine who worked on a copper weld. It was grueling work for men back then, but he managed it by numbing the pain. Faithful to his labor, he served his white-collared masters every day of his life before succumbing to lung cancer at the ripe old age of fifty-four.

Pennsylvania was steeped in the Great Depression. With the steel mills decimating the nation's businesses, America was wilting. Jobs were scarce, and the stifling smog cursed us with its rotting gifts of poverty. We were the pilgrims on a new frontier.

But as the depression waned, my town became full of big city business tycoons, sensible spinsters, and everything in-between. The alleys, bridges, and rivers glued the city together while we kept to traditional values. However, a revolution was underway, birthing a modern society in a blink of an eye. Women were classy, men wore suits, and the hustle-bustle grew abundant with nightlife, theaters, and department stores.

But with all its charisma, Pennsylvania took hits from its unpredictable hot-and-cold climate and cancer from the mills that filled the lungs of neighbors. We held our breaths and sunk our teeth into the new enterprise.

And there were the rest. The outskirts of society—impoverished neighborhoods where gangs, criminals, whores, and other social lepers prowled the byways. Our city had become a parallel universe of ecosystems, like a wild jungle where the alpha males reigned supreme. And underneath its canopy was my childhood home. It was nothing fancy, but it's where my first memories were born.

Amid all that were my parents. They didn't *always* fight. I have memories, glimpses of some good times or simple gestures they would lovingly exchange in the beginning. I believe my father adored my mother. He'd have done anything to please her, but when he fell short, her belittling butchered his ego. I suppose that's where the devil found them alright, behind their misery and the bottle. They kept each other on a chopping block, ridiculing each other's inadequacies and locating the perfect poison to infect their relationship.

Alcoholism took my parents hostage in McKeesport. It chewed them up and spit them out where the drum of the devil's parade beat ferociously a few blocks away. That's where the Brick Alley whorehouse bared its claws and confiscated my father. My mother eventually refused any type of sexual intimacy with him, which drove him to release elsewhere. He wanted his Cora, but she had cut him off in cold blood.

The junction of harlots would gather as my mother pulled up the crooked street. I observed from the back seat, watching the embers of firelight above the smoky city harbor, its guilt and sin festering in one alleyway.

Swallowing her pride, she'd collect payment from each man she dropped off at the whorehouse. Never mind the child (me) in the backseat. In the middle of the night, her taxi transported some of the most prominent men in society (even the mayor), who lived high on the hill—but had her drive them down to the pits of hell. They trusted her alright because Mum was a genius when it came to mastering a stone face in order to increase her earnings.

Many times before, Cora had surrendered Father to the inferno, not batting an eye. I was instructed to keep quiet around neighbors because I had to portray myself as the poster child of America, which meant obeying my parents and minding my own business.

Mum's personality changed because of this, and she became domineering and emotionally distant, perhaps to dull the shame she resented in herself. She was as strong as an ox on the outside, but I could sense an incubator around her heart that kept her from falling to pieces. Her tongue was sharp and her patience thin. Even if it meant food rationing or no heat during the winter, I never complained, for fear she'd strike me. It also didn't help that my father gambled away his earnings, evidenced by the bottles of beer stacking up on the counter. His irresponsibility left us living paycheck to paycheck.

It was hard enough trying to keep up with the both of them, but when Mum suddenly became ill with pneumonia, I was forced to grow up. Shivering at our potbelly stove, I struggled to pour the tomato soup without it scorching my skin. Snickering rodents scurrying behind the walls frightened me as I cradled the bowl of red liquid and gently set it beside her.

Mum looked pale. There, in the twilight, I blew on the soup as I spooned it into her mouth carefully. All the while, the smell of the sickness oozed out her pores and filtered through the room.

A trace of broth trickled down the sides of her lips. I hesitated, watching her labored breathing halt momentarily before the next swallow.

"It's so cold in here." Mum's eyes searched the room.

"I'll warm you, Mummy, don't worry. You're going to get better."

Her arms were as cold as ice. She trembled violently, so I tried to cover her and warm her skin, but she resisted and buried herself under the blanket, leaving me with frayed linens to wrap around my own frozen body.

These memories never really vanished; instead, they swelled.

● ● ●

My parents battled one hardship after the next. Father worked long hours at the steel mill, then after work rewarded himself with a round of drinks. Back at home, the smell of addiction saturated my insides, a pungent stench that overwhelmed my tummy just as the arguments and violence revved up after midnight. My anxious body was jolted awake by the screaming coming from the kitchen.

"Get out of here, all of you!" Cora clutched the kitchen knife in her fists. "You son of a bitch, I'll call the police!" She hurled a glass at my father, trimming the side of his face. It burst on impact.

The mill workers whom my father had invited over had an appetite for my mum—and it was no surprise that he was pawning her off in defiance. The wolf pack moved in closer.

"Aren't you cute when you're mad? Come on, darling, I just want to dance with you." A brawny man with robust features and a scar over his left eye followed her around the dining room table, trying to snatch her.

"I'll slice your throat right open if you come any closer!" She swiped at his neckline, shooing him backward until he lost his balance.

"Well, screw you, you old hag!" he said, trying to get back up.

I peeked a little further around the corner, hoping they wouldn't see me, but one man caught my slipper. Thankfully, I broke away.

"Get in your room and lock the door!" Cora's primal instincts kicked in as she slapped the man across the face.

Refraining from beating her to a bloody pulp, he spit some blood onto the floor and looked at me like a wild animal.

"Don't you look pretty in that blue dress?" he commented, creeping toward me in a drunken dance. But before he could harm me, my father's whistle alerted them to recede. They all stumbled out like vermin, leaving me to run for cover.

Father leaned forward to kiss my mother goodbye.

"You're such an attractive woman, Cora." He hiccupped as he rubbed himself against her pelvis. But before he reached his hand up her dress, she shoved him onto the porch.

"Get out of here, you bastard! It's over!"

• • •

My father's escapades were nothing new. He'd often slip in and out of poor behavior. But once the storm had settled, he'd return and beg for my mother's forgiveness.

"God damn it, Cora! I've promised you that I won't drink again," he'd shout through the blinds while pitching rocks at the curb.

She wouldn't carry a fiddle to his chorus. She'd simply light up a cigarette and gamble on his emotions, ignoring his cries for reconciliation while tending to her chores.

But that night was different. That night she ended it.

"You've never loved me," she said, ripping the cigarette from Martin's mouth. "All you love is yourself!" That's when she decided to toss his clothes outside.

"Just give me another chance." Father's voice receded.

"It's too late, Martin." Mum latched the screen as I peeked around the door. "I've run out of patience loving you. Get the rest of your things tomorrow and get out of my life!"

After the damage was done, there was no rekindling the flame between them. My mother's codependence was the lifeblood of my father's addiction. But that evening, she had cut the umbilical cord and delivered them both.

Days later, my father's truck pulled up the driveway to collect his belongings.

"Don't ever think of coming back here again!" Cora looked like a maniac, fueled with a wicked desire to strangle him dead.

He slammed the driver's side door, avoiding eye contact. He'd ambushed her into an emotional death as he grabbed the last box.

I wrestled to break free from Mum's grasp, watching the truck struggle down the road. But Cora just peered at the trailing exhaust. She looked pleased, then dismissed my tears. She refused to acknowledge my suffering. Vigorously, I pulled at the lining of her coat, begging for them to reconcile. It felt as if the life force were being sucked out of me.

"If you want to go with him, you'll have to run and catch up." She stared off into the distance, interlocked with cruel madness.

Without hesitation, I decided to run as fast as I could until the freezing air stole my breath away. There, in the thick blanket of snow, all that was left were the tracks of my father's truck. Pain perplexed me. If I could bring my father back, everything would be all right.

When I returned home, my brother, Chuck, stood emotionless in the doorway. He was five years older than me. A cruel, husky boy with small, pitched eyes, broad shoulders, and serious brows. All my life, his shrewd displeasure was rampant as he hid his insecurities. I was the antidote to his wrath for years. Behind the scenes, he'd abuse me, emotionally and physically. When we were alone, I became a rag doll for his pleasure since he had become the man of the house. And when I disobeyed, I paid for it. The scars were slow to heal as Cora turned a blind eye. When he'd assault me, it fed his appetite, and he'd continue to slap me until I could no longer form tears. For many years, he was the dominant persecutor at my back.

• • •

Chuck approached me before following Cora's trail into the kitchen. "Father never wanted you, anyway," he snipped. "If he did, he wouldn't have left us."

Overcome with hysteria, I fled up the stairs and pressed my tiny nose against the glass, hoping to see my father's headlights. My palms lay flat against the windowpane as I prayed. I didn't care what devil had taken him—I just wanted him back. That evening, I didn't touch my food or show my shadow.

Be brave. You've got to be! Besides, what Chuck said isn't true. That's how I assured myself as I looked out to a vacant street. *They can't hurt you if you don't let them.*

• • •

A few days later, Father paid us a visit while Cora was at work.

"Hello, Jane." Father patted me on the head like a house pet. "How's Mum doing?" He poked around, hunting for clues.

"Fine, Dad. She's at work right now." I tried to mind my own business.

"Jane, is it true? I heard mother's been seeing someone lately?" He pulled a piece of candy from his pocket to bribe me.

"No one's been over here," I said, looking away.

"OK. Very good. Well, have a nice day at school, Janey, and when you see your mother, let her know I stopped by." He grabbed a slice of crumb cake on his way out the door.

But while he was busy checking on my mother's affairs, we were busy packing and moving. It was just a few miles away, into the crux of the city, into the guts of the 1st Ward slums. Although it was known for its squalor and riffraff, it felt like home. Sure, it was seedy, but when you're a child of poverty, you can't be choosy.

• • •

Now a single, working mother in the slums, Mum spent long nights away, leaving the ruckus of the streets only a stone's throw from our doorstep. I heard the alley dogs, horn-honking, and neighbors shouting profanities across the rooftops while I was trying to say my prayers.

"Are you packed for school tomorrow?" She handed me the laundry basket.

"Yes, but my knuckles won't stop itching!" I'd scratched them relentlessly until they bled.

The next morning, instead of school, she took me to Dr. Fisher, who diagnosed me with impetigo, a highly contagious skin infection that causes red sores on the body. Like a miracle, his special cream worked. Boy, did I have stories to tell at school, referring to him as the marvelous fisherman who saved me from the deep blue sea. I relied on this fabrication because it got me the attention I so desperately desired.

Dr. Fisher stood at just five foot two. He carried a sweet disposition and had a dollop of hair on the center of his otherwise bald head that curled up every time the wind blew through his examination blinds. I'd giggle as he allowed me to smooth each strand.

Funny as it may seem, he was my hero, the only one in the world who looked at me with a smile.

• • •

As Christmas grew closer, it was customary to write a letter to Santa Claus, so I raced home to hand mine to the mailman:

> *Dear Santa,*
> *All I want for Christmas this year is my father back.*
> *Please, I'll be a good little girl. I've completed all my chores,*
> *and Mum and I are getting along! I promise to not cause*
> *any trouble. Please, Santa, please help us!*
> *Jane*

• • •

The Christmas tree lights were perfect. Some didn't work, but it didn't matter. There were lots of gifts under the tree, more than we'd ever seen. Mum's hard work had finally paid off, especially her driving the big rig trucks during World War II.

Chuck raced through his gifts before retiring to his bedroom, where he spent most of his time glued to his comics.

"There's one more back there." Mum pointed. I crawled under and snatched the silver-and-gold present, then unwrapped it quickly. "She's perfect!"

Mum looked pleased. The tiny doll was a miniature replica of me. She was agile and crafted to endure. But as much as I rejoiced in that moment, Santa had ignored my request—my father never returned. I placed my little dolly on the windowsill where she remained for months and where I waited, brokenhearted.

• • •

With the holidays behind us, it felt like Mum's patience was wearing thin. One evening, she was hell-bent on having me serve supper. Irate, she threw me an oven mitt and clenched down on her cigarette.

"Jane, get your ass over here and dish this up for Pete's sake!" She stomped past me in a trail of smoke. "I can't do everything around here to serve you assholes!" Surging with electricity, she headed to the back room where she fiddled with her stockings.

After allowing some time to pass, I carefully peered through the door frame to catch Cora rubbing her feet.

"Mum, can I come in? I'm sorry you've had a bad day today." I cowered to stay unseen.

"Mother's tired right now." She continued braiding her hair while she savored her last cigarette. "Jane, please close the door."

"OK. Well, goodnight."

Suddenly, a hard shove came from behind leaving me breathless. Chuck had been eavesdropping on our conversation.

"Get out of the way, stupid!" He shoved me into the corner. "You're pathetic; you know that? You can't get your stupid face out of everyone's business. It's no wonder Father left us—Mum can't stand you either!" He chugged from the milk carton and wiped his mouth with his sleeve.

I never made eye contact with him, fearing he'd leave more bruises. Mum always forced us to be civil, but the marks of his physical abuse on me weren't easy to ignore.

So here I was caught in the perfect storm. My father was absent, and I was left with a narcissistic mother and a militant teenage brother— the ideal breeding ground for emotional instability. It became the cherry on top of the meatloaf, but I ate it anyway. I was told I was wrong when I was right, but they made the rules, so I kept my mouth shut.

• • •

As the months wore on, the slum yard where we lived had become more and more ravenous with pigeon men, cocked below the belt line with battered egos. Men would come and go inside our apartment; they'd stay a few hours—smoking, drinking, messing around with Cora. She trusted none of them. Her tactic was to use them, booze them, and hurl them curbside. It's a wonder I did so well in school. My grades stayed above average despite living in such a cuckoo nest!

"Jane, can you come here a minute?" Mum said calmly, unclipping her earrings. Curious to see what she had on her mind, I sat patiently as she ran her fingers through my hair. "Never trust men—they're all a bunch of assholes!" She paused, puffing the cig pursed between her lips. "Even Catholics. If you think you've met a saint, you've met the devil!"

She removed her coat with a calculated silence. "I understand I baptized you Catholic, but don't confuse yourself. It's just the men."

She smirked as she turned toward the ashtray. The cigarette burned with intention as I slid under the covers beside her, confused by her borderline personality.

"Mum, then what is Father?" I was apprehensive to ask.

"Irish Catholic, now go to bed!"

After she fell asleep, her words became engraved in my mind. Where were all the civilized men of the world if mother said they're all corrupt? Were they hiding out in orchards? Surely not churches. Where did this American dream really exist?

Chapter 2

SLIM PICKINGS

When I was growing up, my mother pounded her beliefs into my head like a drill bit boring into metal. In the 1930s, families still played an important role in keeping the white-picket-fence dream alive. The portrait of the perfect family was plastered everywhere: television, radio, magazines, billboards. And in Mum's attempt to find Mr. Right, she was determined, especially after learning my father had re-married to a subservient Russian bride.

Mum swore that the best place to find a good listener was at our local pub. Once they were drunk, they were always there to lend her an ear.

But Cora's picks of the litter were characters off a funny farm. Let's see … for starters, there was Stu, Harry, Jasper, Paul, and Smokey. She dated and spat them out one by one like sunflower seeds. After vigilantly trying them on for size, she'd send them back where they came from.

Stu was a respectable man in upper society with fairly good-looking features, but he was as goofy as a wild turkey. He would crack jokes that neither made sense nor made me laugh, yet his sappy grin always looked for confirmation from my mum. His insecurity oozed every time he showed off his horse-like teeth, which I swear were falsies. Cora and Stu dated for a week until she called it quits.

Then there was Harry who was overtly muscular, a thick-haired Roman god with light-blue eyes and a great natural smile. I'll give him that. He was in the process of a divorce and looking for a good time to appease his testosterone levels. Their wild affair gave him an ego boost, but he eventually stopped coming around. It was a no-strings-attached, few-weeks romance that ended when his wife came back into the picture.

After about a month, Cora swore she'd found the one: Jasper. He was stubby, cartoonish looking, with large brown eyes, curly dark hair, and a high-pitched laugh. His gait was even weirder, like he'd thrown back a couple of martinis before each visit.

And he smelled strange too—a mixture of evergreen and old men's cologne. But the real kicker was when I refused to hug him and accidentally stepped on his toes. Boy, did that piss him off. He wanted to send me to boarding school, which didn't sit well with my mum. So, he was toast.

Paul was next in line. He was fascinating. I'll never forget when he told me he was a deep-sea diver. My eyes bugged out. He wasn't only successful—he was incredibly wealthy and wanted to give Mum the world. He charmed her with expensive dinners and gifts ... and even gave me piggyback rides! But in the end, there was nothing he could do to sweep Mum off her feet. Her eyes just didn't light up like they once did with my father.

Paul peeled out of the driveway one evening in a rage, never to return. I think she broke his heart. The caviar was all over the driveway.

It would be a while before another man crossed her threshold. Then one day, I saw her as giddy as a daisy on a string. And that was the day hell's beltway opened and dragged Smokey into our lives.

He was the wild card Cora couldn't shake, a devil in a blue suit who strolled into her heart, blindsiding her with infatuation. He was coy, too hot for his britches, and spoke in clever tongues that only I could translate.

Smokey came knocking on her doorstep like she was a damsel in distress, but Cora was far from that. He knew he had to work for her affections, and no matter what drama unfolded, he won every bet right into her heart.

"Oh, Smokey! How did you know this was my favorite?" She blushed, looking at the piece of pie he brought from the corner bakery. His mouth was sharp and arrogant, but that didn't stop her from putting him on a golden shrine.

Cora had fallen in love with Smokey not just because of his good looks but because he was oddly like her father who had died tragically when she was young. It had been a gruesome accident involving a moving train. He'd lost his grip, and the engine blades severed him in half.

Smokey was the dad my mother never had—and perhaps it rectified him.

Her mother, Stella, had remarried shortly after that to a Bible-preaching, self-righteous nut and gave birth to six of his children while raising two of his from a previous marriage. Well, he did a number on her alright. After his strict rules had brainwashed her, she became a walking-talking debutante, lodged in his ring of fire.

My mother was the black sheep of her family, so I suppose that's where she grew thick skin. We played by the rules—no one played the victim under her authority.

• • •

Maybe it was Smokey's broad shoulders, handsome nose, and the effortless air he courted her with. He must have practiced his lines because he was a real ladies' man. Cora couldn't keep her hands off him.

But as time led on, she began to intervene in his personal affairs, watching his every move like a savage woman hiding in the bushes. That obsession started with the faintest pale lipstick on his collar or her smelling perfume on his clothing when he'd come home from work. She'd accuse him of having affairs, then destroy the house and anything in her path. Unfortunately, I knew when the swearing was over because I'd hear the passionate lovemaking in the back room, which covered his tracks for the time being and made me sick to my stomach.

Back in those days, other kids would tease and ridicule you if your parents didn't live under the same roof. Such was my lot. Classmates disassociated themselves from me at school for having a split family. It provided ammunition for all the bullies who called me everything in the book.

It wasn't a shock. It was just reality. I had to develop the courage to stand up and protect myself, pretend that I was normal even though I wasn't anything but an outcast.

My fists were quick to defend my tiny body. I fought with my head up and endured bloody noses from schoolyard fights—but I walked home with pride, never letting them see me shed a tear.

"Go home and cry to your mommy, little baby!" they'd shout.

"Janey's a bastard baby. No wonder her daddy left her," a group of them howled as they harassed me all the way home. When I made it inside safely, I could breathe again and let the tears fall.

The window facing out to the world was my saving grace whenever I'd see my mum finally coming home from a long night's work. Even though she was too exhausted to say hello, I felt at ease when she was there.

• • •

"Bundle up now. It's cold outside." She gripped my zipper, yanking it up.

"How far is it, Mum?" I was already trembling from the frigid draft.

"Not far. Just walk past the park and over the bridge. You'll go about two blocks from the mill house. The pub will be on your right, but don't talk to strangers. If anyone asks who you're looking for, just tell them you're looking for Fish."

"I'm afraid I'll get lost," I said, shivering in the doorway. Mid-evening was just around the corner.

"When you find him, tell him you and your brother need money—or you'll be without a roof over your heads! Now hurry, before it gets dark!" She patted me on the bottom and shooed me outside.

Money had become scarce when she lost work. I knew it was only a matter of time before she'd ask me to head to the bars and beg Father for rent money.

With one foot ahead of the next, I finally reached the pub, just as she had instructed. The sunset was receding as I squeezed through the crowd. I hurried along, pulling on the pant legs of grown men. I was a child in an adult playground.

The bar was loud and filled with grimy mill workers satisfying their appetites on young flesh.

"Is Fish here?!" I wailed over the music, cowering to keep a low profile.

"No, he's not, little girl, but I'll be your daddy." The man stretched out his fingers—he was like a serpent from hell—to fondle my hair. I pushed the stranger away and hid in the corner waiting for signs of my father.

As the night carried on, the ashtrays filled with smoky soot. The clanging mugs and beguiled laughter salted the space with negative energy and a sense of danger. Clumsily, I made my way out into the alleyway with nothing to show for my efforts.

I stumbled through the door after practically losing feeling in my legs.

"How's the old man?" Chuck gave a hissing laugh.

"He wasn't there," I said, removing my snow-drenched coat.

"Pitiful! You'll disappoint Mum." Oh, how he relished my defeat.

The snow on my toes slowly melted as I warmed my feet by the fire. As I got into bed, I trained myself to move to the far edges of the mattress that Mum shared with Smokey. In the wee hours of dawn, I could hear them make love beside me. Disgusted, I pressed the pillow as hard as I could over my head and prayed to God to make it all go away.

The only distraction I had was the wind against the glass, blowing loudly to block out the insanity I was living under. Eventually, I fell asleep, but it had imprinted on my mind.

• • •

Mum continued to pawn me off, and it was my duty to collect the rent each month from Father. No more feelings, no more emotions, just an attitude of survival and the wits to outsmart grown men from harming me as I searched for his whereabouts. I ached and converted the trauma to desperation. I'd go to any lengths to mend my family. In a last attempt, I walked into the bar to find him.

"Father, it's Jane," I said, catching my breath. "Mother sent me to find you. She needs more money—it wasn't enough last month, and we'll be evicted if we're late."

He looked through me as if I were a ghost.

"You can't be in here, Jane. Tell your mother to sort out her own goddamn shit." He sipped slowly, trying to ignore my presence. However, my heart kept beating with resilience, wondering if somehow, I could bribe him.

As I waited for a response, I realized that he wasn't at all curious about me, only the wench across the way that enticed his thirst.

"Your mum needs to find you a new daddy, Jane." He winked back at the woman. My heart fell unconscious.

"If you won't come home, please just give us a little more so we can keep the roof over our heads," I demanded, building up the courage to bargain with him.

"Come by the house tomorrow, then. I'll see what I can spare." He got up and left me behind.

On the long walk home, I chewed my pride as I forced myself to hold back the tears. The air stung my eyes, but I kept them glued to the dark alleys. I could hear rats tinkering in the dumpsters and pockets of branches cracking underneath my feet, but it wasn't more terrifying than realizing I was without a father indefinitely.

Chapter 3

A Little Piece of Heaven -
A Whole Lot of Hell

When you feel alone in the world, it's difficult to let anyone inside. If I did, it was because I thought I could trust them.

Gloria and Dorothy were two acquaintances from school. Both girls were raised in stable households and had a wealth of family stories to share—stories about Sunday dinners and weekend getaways that had me wishing I was them. Gloria was soft-spoken and dreamed of becoming a model, after auditioning for ads in the local newspaper. Her features were perfectly in proportion, along with her statuesque height.

Dorothy was heavyset with dimples. She talked with her bright blue eyes and was an excellent seamstress. Customary to her German-Italian heritage, she could cook, which would land her a career right out of high school as the recipe guru for her husband's restaurant.

When we were young, we fantasized about womanhood, the boys we crushed over, and movie stars. We spent weekends swapping ghost stories, watching horror movies, and battling through puberty. Our bodies were changing, but our minds were childlike. There was a zest for freedom and no limits as we roller-skated to our favorite songs, dolled ourselves up like Doris Day, and stuffed our bras with toilet tissue.

Those days were worth living it up. We could talk for hours and escape to the river during the hot summers, hang at the movies, and run around Kennywood amusement park after sundown. The humidity from the long summers kept me awake at night. While I waited for sleep to come, I'd anticipate lacing up the next day and escaping Mother's leash so I could skinny-dip in the river. There was a freedom before childbearing that made us feel untouchable.

Every year on my birthday, I blew out my candles wishing to reunite with my father. But I began to realize that we were only a transaction in his new life. He seemed a million miles away, even though he was only across the bridge.

• • •

One evening, Dorothy and I spent the night at Gloria's.

"Do you believe people can get back together?" I asked as we hudâled in our sleeping bags.

"Of course, I do!" Gloria's voice piqued with enthusiasm.

"Why aren't your mother and father together anymore?" Dorothy shot me a somber look.

"They don't get along." I ignored my friends for a moment and stared out the window at the night sky, haunted by the truth.

Dorothy removed her retainer. "I don't understand; your parents seem so perfect."

"That's the problem, you guys. Everything isn't always perfect."

"Let's not talk about this anymore; it's time to go to sleep," Gloria whispered as she turned off the light.

"Goodnight." We hugged our pillows and escaped to dreamland.

• • •

During my adolescent years, Mum moved us once again, this time to 10th Ward Pennsylvania, 416 W 5th Avenue. I was in the same district, and the stigma followed me wherever I went.

While my girlfriends were enjoying bonding time with their families, I was unpacking, thinking about how I'd leave this town someday.

"I'll be back later!" I shouted, as I laced up and skated down the street. Faster and faster, I pushed, whisking past old estates and mill yards, pulling vines from neighbors' fences. Life on the other side of 10th Street meant hope—my light at the end of the tunnel, a reprieve for starting over.

And once I reached the hilltop, just before the sunset slipped away, I shouted to the Gods of the Universe "I'm on top of the world!!!" My voice echoed over the town as if I'd defeated Goliath.

Exhilarated by the scenery below, I worked to catch my breath. "Alright, time to head home."

Over the years that would come and go, my only defense was to depend on myself and not on others. My mind escaped into a time machine that took me on many adventures.

• • •

Whenever the weather was muggy indoors, I'd spend hours by the riverbed. It was more bearable than living under Mother's roof and Smokey's laziness.

He'd gained a few pounds from her pot roast dinners and poked his nose in everyone's business. His sexist nature pestered me. He'd spend his days lounging on our furniture and sweating through the sheets. But Cora protected him, cleaned up his messes, and massaged his ego, even after she'd had a hard day's work.

Why a woman like my mother would tolerate a man like Smokey baffled me. She took pride in everything she did. Although the walls were caving in and spider webs dressed the hallways, she'd stand on her tippy toes to swat them down. She couldn't afford much, but she earned every penny she had.

"Money is the root of all evil, Jane." She placed the broom behind the door. "It can run a gamut of emotions in men's heads. Provoke things in people that make them do crazy things." She wiped the sweat from her brow. "But it can also spare you a hard life, and one day you'll cherish that paper trail in your bank account for keeping you alive."

She untucked her blouse before retiring to the kitchen sink and removing the dirt from her hands.

"When you scrub a floor, you don't just mop it, you get down on your hands and knees," she said, drying off her palms.

I smiled, mesmerized by her allegiance.

Mum had tied up the loose ends when she washed up. She was thankful for her small success, even though she cursed at the street birds who turned their noses up at her. Every quarter mattered, and she was right when she taught us survival skills. Money makes people do crazy things, and I learned it all from her.

• • •

The first of the month was approaching and rent was due. Any moment, our landlord would pay us a visit—usually when Mum was home. But this time, I had to take matters into my own hands. We didn't have the rent money, and time had run out.

The Oldsmobile coming up the street tilted to one side of the road, as our landlord struggled to exit the driver's seat. Out of breath and barely alive, he swung open our porch screen as I hid behind the curtains.

He pounded on the door. "I know you're in there! Open up!" he said with a thick Italian accent.

Through the crack of the blinds, I could see him suck up the saliva dribbling from his cigar.

"You sons of bitches, trying to mess with me!" His morbidly obese frame pressed against the door to peek through the crack. His eyeballs looked like orange skins.

"You're two weeks late! Either you open the door, or I'll leave this eviction notice!" He grabbed a rag from his trousers to wipe his forehead.

But before he could say another word, I grew the bravery to confront him and let him have it.

"You listen to me, Mr. Landman! The city shut off our lights again, so I'm doing my homework by candlelight, and the wax stuck my pages together, and you know what's even better?" I paused. "Some asshole kid at school broke my glasses, so I can't see the blackboard! And if you don't get the hell off our porch, I'm going to scream bloody murder, so this entire town will think you're murdering me!"

The chirping of the birds suddenly stopped as his angry brows turned upside down in bewilderment. He retracted like a wobbly flamingo tripping over a sprinkler cap and landed on his bottom.

"Your mother better pay the rent, or I'll evict all of you! Capisci?" His face turned bright red. "Madonna, Che Palle!" he muttered under his breath, as he leveraged himself back onto his legs and limped away like a wounded animal.

"Capisco!" I hollered back, slamming the door shut.

I was shaking uncontrollably afterward, but I was certain Mum would give me a medal.

• • •

"I hope you're happy!" Mum slammed the rental notice on the table. "He raised our rent five dollars."

"He wanted to evict us, Mum! Don't you realize how brave I was to confront him? You should have seen his face!"

"It's not always about being brave, Jane. It's about knowing when to keep your mouth shut!" She grabbed me by the shoulders to shake some sense into me.

"Then why are you always so bold?" I stepped back to glare at her.

"You're a child! You haven't seen the world like I have." She turned with a swift jerk to head to her bedroom.

"Then why am I the one you send into the world to look for Father?" I challenged her, before holding my tongue.

She turned with rage and smacked me across the face, leaving a welt over my eye.

"Shut your mouth! I don't ever want to hear you bring him up in this house again! Do I make myself clear?"

My body felt paralyzed. I choked back my pride as she looked repulsed by my presence. The actress had lost the performance. Cora always won and made me feel beneath her.

• • •

A few days later, I arrived at Father's doorstep to be greeted by his wife, Helen, who was drunk on brandy. She opened the door and examined me like I was trash.

"We don't have any money, Janey. Go home to your mother!" She cackled, seemingly entertained by my desperation. "Doesn't Cora have enough men to pay her wages?"

The brittle cold had seeped into my shoes and coat pockets, as I stood waiting for a savior. My life was a little piece of heaven mixed in with a whole lot of hell. I screamed up at the stars as I made my way back; leaving empty-handed was a bitter pill to swallow.

As I approached the dimly lit windows of home, I turned the knob carefully to remain undetected. The putrid air of cigarettes and burned roast kidnapped my senses as I removed my clothing and slipped into my pajamas. Routinely I stuffed my ears with toilet tissue just to block out Cora and Smokey's sex acts. There was nowhere to escape but to my dreams.

I would reincarnate myself many times in my life, using the skills inherited from my DNA to forge my name until it made sense. Whether I'd become Bette Davis, Jean Harlow, or Doris Day, I was a force to be reckoned with. But at least I learned from the best.

The 1940s brought amazing changes. We had new inventions and modern kitchen appliances. It was a step in the right direction and a step closer to overcoming Cora's dirty laundry and my father's absence.

Growing older meant confronting my insecurities and getting the answers I'd always wanted. It led me to confront my father and get the closure I desperately needed.

Chapter 4

SPIRITUAL DARKNESS

*"When the only self-respect you have is your sacred space, and
someone invades your body, you become a vapor. You can filter the sin,
but you can't wash it clean. I forgave because I know man is sinful.
He can't help himself. The Lord has taught me to forgive."*

— JANE CORSARO

In Pennsylvania, it's painful when it's cold outside, but even more when you break your leg using a fire escape down an icy pole.

Taking risks was a habit of mine, especially when it got my mother's attention. When the accident happened, I was alone, but thankfully a neighbor heard me call out. That's right. The entire town heard me holler from Timbuktu once my ankle broke.

"For God's sake, Jane, why are you always causing trouble?" Cora pressed the ice pack on my swollen leg as I bit down on the washcloth. She'd never cursed this much, but today was the exception. I think she used every curse word known to man.

As we rushed to the doctor, Cora weaved around pedestrians and almost caused an accident while barely missing Mrs. Emerson, the morbidly old librarian who could barely walk.

"Keep the ice on your leg!" she demanded, trying to steer and hold me still.

"Son of a bitch!" I cursed, barely missing a slap on the back of the head, only because she took pity on me.

"Now you'll learn not to slide down poles!"

Once the doctor set my ankle and placed a cast from the top of my leg down to my toes, I looked ready for Halloween. It took practice balancing on crutches, especially getting in and out of the car. The only thing I could glorify was the guts it took to slide down the pole in the first place.

For three miserable months, Cora kept me on restriction. The only things allowed were homework and chores. She enjoyed reminding me how foolish I was every time she saw me sticking wire hangers in my cast to ease the itching.

"You're just like your father." She shot me a persuasive glance before turning the pages of her magazine. "I'm warning you now, if you don't straighten up, Jane, I'm going to send you to boarding school."

I always heard her ultimatums loud and clear, even though I pretended not to pay any attention. If she sent me away, it probably would have been a blessing—at least I wouldn't have to share a room with her and Smokey.

"I spoke with Grandma Quinn today, and I'll be dropping you off tomorrow afternoon." She closed the magazine to fix supper.

"What for? I'm sorry for what I did."

"Never mind your apologies; it will be good for the both of us." Cora started the burner, content with her decision.

"Grandma Quinn?" I whined.

She was a stranger to me. I'd been raised hearing stories about all of them, especially about my beautiful aunts, Marie and Mildred. Supposedly, they lived with my grandmother. The spotless mansion was a palace built for royalty, one of the finest in town.

The next morning, just as Cora had promised, I was off. My crutches buckled as I hobbled up the stone walkway to the distinguished Colonial. Cora dug her fingers into my back as she trailed behind me.

"Keep quiet and remember to smile graciously." She tugged at my arm.

"Yes, Mum."

Cora wasn't close to any of her relatives, but when she needed a favor, she knew that Grandma Quinn would crack the door wide enough to fulfill my mother's desperate pleas.

The doorbell's trumpet sent shivers up my body. As the door opened to an exquisite foyer, a stern-looking woman with bushy gray brows and a frown for a smile greeted us.

"Hello, Jane. You've really grown up, haven't you?" she said, spinning me around to see where I'd fit best among her things.

Cora, on the other hand, refrained from coming inside. She exchanged only a nod with Grandma Quinn, in return for her accommodations. After a minute of priming me, she retreated to the car as I reluctantly waved goodbye, looking for a way to escape.

"Jane, is that you?" two wind-up toy voices chimed behind me.

"Look! She has her father's eyes!" Aunt Marie pushed my chin higher than it could tilt. "Cora never told us you were a looker." Her vindictive hospitality made me gag as she gazed into my eyes like a cobra.

"Thank you." I shuffled backward, trying to remain pleasant.

"Such a beautiful child," Mildred said, balancing a ripe peach between her fingers.

Aunt Marie reminded me of a princess, with velvety soft skin, a long swanlike neck, and a curvy physique with spindles of curls falling at her waistline. Mildred was a mysterious beauty, blessed with high cheekbones and romantic eyes that strived for perfection. I admired my aunts' poise and stature, but underneath their demure appearances was a nakedness.

"You must be tired. Go ahead and get washed up for supper," Aunt Marie said, following Grandma Quinn and Mildred into the kitchen.

I could hear them talking, so I pressed my ear against the wall.

"Well, well, well. Jane is here for the weekend—I bet you didn't expect that," one of the sisters said.

"That's right. Cora dropped her off so she can go whoring around," the other answered, followed by a wicked laugh.

"Such a shame. She'll probably grow up to be just like her," Grandma Quinn's voice muttered boldly.

Abruptly, and before I could satisfy my rage, I headed for the door.

"Where are you going, honey?" Aunt Marie stood in the parlor, forcing a fake smile.

I bit my lower lip, stopping myself from clawing out her eyes.

"I realized I left some homework back home," I said.

"Are you sure you want to walk? It's so windy outside. At least take some money for the bus." She handed over some pocket change.

"No, thank you. I'll manage." I closed my hand around hers to refuse her offering.

That afternoon, I left, never to return. I made my way down the garden and stopped after a few yards to take in the view of my slum on the horizon. The reality, although scary, was at least honest—not like Grandma Quinn's house full of illusions.

When I reached home, I made my way inside, trying not to distract Cora.

"What are you doing home so soon?" Her eyes struck me.

"I forgot my homework," I said, hoping she'd take pity on me.

"Well, don't stand in the doorway; come inside and wash up." She raised her voice while returning to her stew. "Dinner will be ready shortly."

That evening before bed, I could hear the trees battering the neighborhood, as the passing cars splashed through the puddles.

It had been a long winter, but when it was over, good news finally came. The doctor removed my cast, and Cora took me off restriction. I saved all the change from my chores, proudly storing it in my piggy bank. It was only two dollars, but back then, it could buy you movie tickets and a ton of candy at the local market.

• • •

One afternoon after school, Chuck startled me while I was gathering my things.

"Whatcha doing, Janey?" He gazed at me with fire in his eyes.

"Nothing, Chuck. I'm just getting ready for the movies."

"The movies? Who said?" His eyes narrowed as he approached.

"Mum said, as long as I pay my own way."

I could feel his breath at the back of my neck.

"Oh, really? So, where's this secret stash?" He looked around obsessively, lifting the covers and tearing the room apart.

I became frantic and pushed up against his heavy frame which was blocking me.

"Chuck, come on! I need to get going, or I'll be late!"

"You're not going anywhere until you tell me where it is." He pushed me across the room, ripping a seam of my dress. "Where is it?"

His eyes burned through mine like hot coals until I had no other choice. I pointed to the corner of my bedside where the tiny piggy bank sat behind Mum's sewing box.

Chuck laughed with victory. "You're stupid! I can't believe you just told me where you hide your loose change."

"No, Chuck! Please!" I charged at him, clawing his shirt.

"Get your hands off me, you pathetic little brat!" He pulled my hair with a swift jerk, then started pouring the coins into his hands.

"If you ever tell Mum about this, I'll get you worse next time!" He threw the piggy bank at the wall, crushing it on impact.

Frightened, I shut my eyes and fell to my knees, slowly picking up the tiny pieces.

"Clean it up before she comes home," he barked.

My body trembled as I quickly discarded the broken glass, paralyzed with fear that he'd return. I shoved the bag at the base of the trash and canceled my plans with Gloria, whom I had promised to meet at the theater that evening.

I became his victim and dove into a spiritual darkness. God seemed distant in this time of desperation, but somehow, I knew he wouldn't leave me behind.

"You can't come over anymore, Jane." Gloria and Dorothy looked knee-deep in guilt.

"Besides, every time we invite you anywhere, you never show up."

"You both know why," I said, trying to defend myself.

"Well, we both agreed that maybe you need to patch things up with your family. Everyone's talking about you, and it's making us uncomfortable. We can't always cover up for you or the bruises."

At that moment I realized our friendship had run its course. It felt like vinegar on a fresh wound. It stung, but eventually, it healed.

• • •

A few days later, Chuck assaulted me once again after he forced me to clean his room. I remember looking into the bathroom mirror and wiping the dried blood from my eyelids.

"What the hell is the matter with you two?" Cora raged, throwing the groceries on the countertop.

"Jane slapped me, and when I pushed her to defend myself, my hand slipped and my ring cut through the skin," he argued as he helped her unpack.

"Not true, Mum! He's lying!"

"I don't have time for this nonsense. Clean yourselves up for supper and quit the dramatics!"

• • •

After dinner on the eve of my thirteenth birthday, I wasn't feeling very well. My stomach cramped like mad, and I could feel the thrust of something pelting my back and lower pelvic muscles. I pushed back my chair at the dining table and hurried to the bathroom. It was clear something strange was going on.

After cleaning up, I looked down at the blood-soiled toilet paper swirling in the water. I leaned over in panic, watching it stain the water.

Cora tapped on the door.

"Not now!" I raised my voice.

She'd told me about periods but never prepared me for them. I sulked, sitting on the bathroom toilet lid. First, I got breasts and acne, and now this. It was all happening too quickly for me to wrap my head around. Overnight, I had joined the millions of female swine in a world of wild boars!

"Are you OK?" Mum whispered.

I opened the door, and she slipped inside discreetly. Her face softened when she peeked inside the toilet.

"Welcome to womanhood, Jane." She sounded like a wolf in sheep's clothing, knowing all along my period was a curse.

Her normal thick-skinned demeanor relaxed when she served me chamomile tea for my abdominal cramps. However, the pain amplified when I moved. I tossed and turned, poking at my pelvis most of the night.

The next morning, the pain had subsided, leaving me with a glimpse of optimism. Maybe this meant I would survive womanhood after all. But with this change others grew jealous. Girls became contentious with each other, like a nest of seagulls looking for mates. No matter how old I got, women took me as a threat.

Society raised us to fill the shoes of our mothers. It was customary to marry before you were eighteen and have children before you were twenty. We had to dismiss our big dreams because the men who ran our households squashed them.

"Jane, didn't you hear?" One of my classmates tapped my shoulder.

"Hear what?"

"Donna wants to fight you in the schoolyard after class!" Her voice cracked.

"Ladies, are you paying attention?" Miss Rasmussen scowled at us impatiently.

"How do you know that?" I asked, starting to watch the clock earnestly.

"I heard it at recess. Everyone's been talking about how she's going to lay one into you for looking at her boyfriend. You better prepare yourself—she's the size of my dad!"

"Don't worry about me. I'll find a way to outrun her." I shrugged, looking for a way to escape.

Before I could place my pencil on the desk, the school bell rang like the tone of a boxing match. Tripping over myself, I bolted for the door.

"Not so fast!" Miss Rasmussen's arm pressed into my chest.

"Yes, Miss Rasmussen?" I perked up to avoid her glare.

"Why are you in such a rush? I've noticed you've been very restless lately. Would you like to talk about it?"

She leaned in like a badger.

"I'm fine. I have a lot of chores to do at home and haven't been sleeping much. Anyhow, I really need to get going, if you'll excuse me?" I pushed my way through the door with a complacent smile, then made a run for it.

"See you tomorrow," she said, as I scurried down the hallway, out the doors, into the schoolyard, and right into Donna's trap, bumping into her gut.

She towered over me like a giant praying mantis. Her mouth watered with excitement while the schoolyard bloodhounds cheered in delight.

"Hello, Donna." I gulped.

"Hello nothing!" She spit at my face. "They tell me you're interested in Jimmy?" she yelled, throwing the first punch into my jaw.

Then she pounded her fists together and came closer for a second knockout.

"Come on, Baby Jane, get up!" She looked down, ready to dig her heel into my ribs.

Donna was just like my brother. She was thicker than lard, brawny and muscular, with long dishwater hair and a stump for a nose.

"Are you ready for more?"

The schoolyard howled wildly like adolescent banshees.

"Come on, Donna! Give it to her! Give her something to cry about!"

Dizzy, I rose to my feet, wiping the blood from my lip and grinning back at her. It was now or never, so I charged her, using every bit of force to knock her down, but I was a twig compared to her strength.

Donna's eyes felt like daggers penetrating my nervous system. She swung around and jabbed me in the eye, knocking me back onto the cement like a piñata, blown to smithereens.

She was wildly jealous, and although Jimmy and I were only friends, she wanted me dead.

I struggled to stand, feeling as if my legs would give out. Every inch of my body burned with pain, but a voice inside me forced me to stand. She began circling me like a tiger, but I lifted my head and held my stance with an uncomfortable silence.

Nothing could harm or devour me—if I showed no fear. It was my victory in the end. I dusted off my dirty hands and left Donna under the orange sky that afternoon. Once she realized I wouldn't fight back, I had won the battle—and she had lost the war.

"What on earth? What happened today?" Mum's eyes calibrated as I entered.

"Nothing happened. I don't want to talk about it!" I slammed the bathroom door. Sedated by the pain, I licked my wounds and realized the world was a human battlefield.

"Jane?"

When I opened the door, Mum was cradling the door frame and looking for answers. I was too embarrassed to look at her, so I stared at the floor tiles.

"I'm proud of you for standing up for yourself," Mum asserted.

That evening I couldn't sleep, fearing that Donna was making plans for my funeral.

However, the anxiety quickly dissipated the moment we made eye contact the next day in the hallway.

"Morning, Jane!" Donna shouted over the chaos. "I have a few things for you." With a nervous grin, she handed me some school supplies.

"What's this?" I said, confused by her generosity.

"Just a few items I wanted you to have. Here, take them. There's a notebook, pencils, and a bunch of other supplies you might like."

Donna looked over her shoulder, wavering in guilt. Miss Rasmussen had been watching us closely.

"Listen, you won't say anything, will you?" She bit her upper lip until the pink turned bright red. Suddenly, she was at my mercy, but after a few indulgent moments, I felt it was punishment enough.

"About what?" My eyes squinted to remind her.

I saw the apology shift in her expression. Apparently, my response had taken her by surprise.

"You can keep your school supplies. I'm sure there's someone who needs them more than I do."

That day the heroine in me prevailed. Donna was left with a life lesson to never mess with wisdom.

• • •

Growing up forced me to choose sides between the Bible and the local fashion column. Advertisements and false prophets came by the truck-loads, and if you weren't reading your Bible, you were undoubtedly serving the devil. I knew about God and prayed every chance I could, but with Cora's cursing on Sundays, it made me question my chances of ever being saved.

Life's hardships helped me carry my crosses and bury my losses. When the neighbors gossiped at night, you had to dig a six-foot ditch behind you, praying whatever was following would fall by the wayside. Call it superstition, but it was a real nail-biter when the community placed a target on your back. The only way to God was to walk by faith and not by sight. So that's what I did from that point onwards.

• • •

When the morning dew hit the windowpane, I awoke energized. The spring flowers gave off a new scent, changing my perception and birth-ing passion in my teenage heart.

I couldn't wait to get to the amusement park. Kennywood was the land of hormones. It was where all the school kids went to hook up. But not me; I was too shy to make a first move.

For three hours, I waited for Marlon—an acquaintance from school—to pick me up from the bus stop, but when she never arrived, I finally realized she'd forgotten me. Sweating under the blistering sunlight, I became an afternoon snack for the mosquitos.

Marlon's mother was a bona fide debutante, and her father was an industrial bigwig. She always dressed impeccably, while I offered to take her hand-me-downs. We were from two different worlds.

• • •

As I walked home, men with wagging tongues honked and whistled as they drove by. The weather in late spring meant braving the humidity, hunkering down in a melting pot, and laying ice packs across every square inch of my body.

I'd saunter past the oak trees and daydream about the enchantment of Kennywood, the sweet smell of caramel apples, and the fluffy cotton candy spun around my fingers. I could almost taste the sugar melt in my mouth. And I'd imagine the feel of my first kiss on my lips and a soft breeze carrying us away—that is until I choked on the aftertaste of exhaust pipes.

• • •

Monday morning, when we returned to school, Marlon was waiting for me.

"I'm sorry, Jane, but we can't hang out anymore." She avoided making eye contact. "Mother says it's not good for me to hang out with girls like you."

She pulled the lipstick from her purse and puckered up, inflating her ego, which was the size of a hot-air balloon. When the lunch bell sounded, she popped her bubble gum and pranced away on her heels as if I had never existed.

Henry, the school know-it-all, startled me by pinching my arm.

"Marlon said you were under the bridge with boys yesterday fooling around!"

"Not so fast," I said, grabbing him by his collar before he could run down the hallway. "What did she say?"

Henry's icy-blond hair and piercing-blue eyes spared him from ever getting in trouble, although he was a pest when it came to stirring up gossip.

"Marlon's been telling everyone that you're not a virgin! You're not a virgin?" He looked astonished and oddly amused.

I could see Marlon giggling at the far end of the hallway. My face turned violet with rage as I ran to the principal's office to escape the embarrassment. But before I could enter, the dean grabbed me and catapulted me into her chair.

"What's this I'm hearing, Jane? All this talk of boys and a rendezvous under the bridge?" The dean paced back and forth, watching my every move. "Miss Rasmussen says you're a frivolous girl who's always looking for trouble. Girls like you are what give other young ladies a poor reputation." She slammed down her pen to turn down the blinds.

Marlon's lie had butchered my name. I hung my head shamefully.

Her voice grew bitter. "Jane, I wasn't born yesterday. I know a woman's desires can tarnish her good reputation. Do you want to corrupt your name?"

"No. That's not what I want. They're just rumors!"

But it was my word against theirs.

"Well, Jane, I believe there is truth to those rumors; that's why I am admitting you to juvenile hall. We've already contacted your mother. Collect your things." She turned to dismiss me.

As I waited outside her office, I could see Miss Rasmussen on the phone.

She scanned me up and down like a laser, disrobing my conscience. I heard her say, "She won't be able to return until she cleans up her act."

I broke down hysterically once I saw Cora storming through the door, certain she would never believe me.

"Don't say a word!" she warned me as she signed off on the papers issued by the school board. "Not one word, do you hear me?" She dug her nails into my skin, holding me in line until she dropped me off at juvenile hall.

• • •

My lips trembled. I was fixed to the observation chair, watching the warden's eyes dissect me. But the cold draft coming from the broken shaft of the admission cell was even worse.

"Remove your clothes." The warden held her baton firmly like a weapon ready to strike.

Shaking uncontrollably, my jaw locked, and my knees froze shut.

"Take off your clothes!" she yelled into my ear.

Angrier than the sin of all hell, I took one last look at Cora, as they all watched me undress. My last garment fell to the floor, exposing my tan lines and bony legs. The warden pulled a scope from her exam table and handcuffed me. I resisted with all my might, locking my legs tightly together as she wrestled with another warden to yank them apart.

"No!" I screamed.

"Hold her still!" the woman pushed against me.

I grunted and struggled as she inserted the instrument into my privates.

"Don't move!" she warned, treating me as if I were a science project experiment.

As they pulled the scope out, the stress made me vomit.

"She's still a virgin," the warden said out loud. They placed the scope on the table and removed their gloves.

My body felt violated and inhuman. There was nothing to hide anymore. My innocence was butchered.

"You can gown up."

I felt like a soured piece of meat. The worst part was feeling dirty, as if I had committed a sin. No matter how hard I scrubbed in the shower, I couldn't get the scent of metal off my skin.

When I finally returned to school, I remained a leper. The gossip had passed, but the shackles remained a reminder of what damage was done. My own mother ignored it, so the shame of feeling impure followed me.

Those bastards took my virginity.

Humans, when they don't operate with two cents, are like weapons. After they claimed my body, I could no longer feel fear. It was a silent invasion of privacy and pain all at once. I'd never fear again.

Chapter 5

GROWING PAINS

> *"From spiritual darkness to a road map that would lead me
> to grace, I took my courage to new heights. People would respect
> my strength. They would feel my will to survive. The living God
> inside me was enough, and an armor merged with my spirit to create
> a character so determined, I would fight hell storms to endure defeat.
> That's when the spiritual darkness vanished, and I was more alive
> than ever. They just hadn't met this side of me yet. When my past
> almost incarcerated me, I overcame it with forgiveness."*

—JANE CORSARO

There is a first for everything, whether it's a scary life circumstance or the most monumental time in a girl's life—her first kiss. The growing pains of early adulthood are there to shape you and realize the secrets and mysteries of people who reveal their true colors.

During my last year of high school, I dated David, my first boyfriend. All the girls thought he was a dream, but I was hardly smitten. He was a big-shot wrestler in high school—that's how he built his reputation. On paper, we looked like the perfect match. But the only thing we had in common was our class schedule.

Our relationship was as quick-lived as a round of wrestling. David worshiped his ego, and, after an accident involving ketchup on my T-shirt, it was obvious we weren't going to walk down the aisle anytime soon.

"Jane, I can't walk you to class today," he whispered in my ear.

"Why not?" I looked him over while removing the ketchup stain.

David lifted his chin honorably, trying to brush off his embarrassment.

"Jane, they're laughing at us. Clean yourself up and we'll go for a soda later. OK?"

"I'll tell you what would be nice," I said, forcing a smile. "Why don't you take your reputation somewhere else and leave me out of it? I'm not interested in you or your skinny chicken legs. We're finished!"

Poor David. His reputation was never the same after that. He tried apologizing, but I'd already written him off like the cafeteria lunch stamp. My tenacity was as artful as the ketchup design on my T-shirt, and everyone knew it. Once I was done, I was done!

• • •

High school was a circus. When you're a sixteen-year-old girl, it feels like an eternity waiting to go around again. So, in the meantime, thanks to color television, I promised myself I'd marry Elvis and sail around the world. I must have driven Mum crazy when I kept refusing offers to the school dances, but I wasn't interested in anyone.

Well … until I met Ray. When I first laid eyes on him, my heart shot from here to the moon. Butterflies filled my stomach, and I couldn't resist his affection. Mum warned me that would happen, but I didn't realize it would feel like this.

Ray was incredibly handsome. His dark black hair and muscular build went perfectly with his amber eyes and handsome smile. Every girl swooned over him, which made him a high-grade heartthrob in my book.

That school year, I'd made friends with Geraldine, whose boyfriend was Ray's close friend on the school baseball team. He'd just moved from Illinois and was settling into our small town. Geraldine was spunky, full of charm, and outspoken. You could never keep her quiet. She was bold and quirky, a beauty in tomboy clothing and the spitting image of Barbara Stanwyck.

Every summer, we soaked up the sunshine any chance we could, layering ourselves with tanning lotion and paying dearly for our sunburns.

The first weekend of summer was when Ray waltzed into my life.

"Hello, ladies," he said, towering over us. But all I could see was his silhouette blocking the afternoon sun.

"Hello." I smiled, making sure my bikini top was secured.

Geraldine fixed her sunglasses, irritated by his abrupt arrival. "I thought you and Richard wouldn't be back till later?"

"Who's your friend?" Ray slipped a piece of gum into his mouth.

"Oh, sorry. This is Jane. She lives down the street."

"Have we met? You look familiar," he said, raising his sunglasses.

"No, I don't think we have." I blushed as he helped me to my feet.

Richard threw his car keys onto Geraldine's towel. "Sorry it took me so long." He turned to Ray. "I see you and Jane have met." He grabbed Ray's shoulder to congratulate him.

"Hey! I have a great idea. Why don't we all go to the movies tonight?"

Geraldine shrieked while throwing herself onto his lap. "That sounds swell!"

"I'm in." Ray winked.

"Sure, me too."

Every chance he could, Ray charmed me with his exotic good looks and stories of his travels. But even better was the first time he kissed me. I was so nervous that I almost choked on my popcorn. I could tell he was a professional alright because of the way he caressed my face and made me feel delicate in his presence.

Ray made it easy for me to fall for him. We would kiss for hours, stroll hand in hand, and dance to our favorite songs under the old oak trees with the radio blaring from the car. It was an innocent playground, sweet and savory, but it ended in the blink of an eye. Just as young hearts burn with fire, they can fizzle without warning.

Ray showed me what love and heartbreak felt like that summer. We were out of control, strapped to our fantasies and living without boundaries. We shared our last kiss—my cherry-flavored Chapstick nearly welding us together as the summer's monsoon moisture dripped down our skin. He waved goodbye, driving away in Richard's old Chevy pickup truck. It was the last time I would see him.

A few weeks later, I found out he'd moved away. Though I was heartbroken and hell-bent on hating every man alive, I somehow found gratitude. If there was one thing to be remembered from our short-lived romance, it was that he was a great kisser—and that's what I was going to miss the most.

Geraldine painted her nails aimlessly as I cursed over the loud music.

"That jerk didn't even send me a letter!" I said, tossing a magazine across the side of the bed before taking a look at the mascara streaking down my face.

"There will be others, Jane. Besides, it's only because he was your first kiss. My mother tells me that all the time. It's always your first that leaves you the most brokenhearted."

Geraldine smothered on her lipstick just as Richard honked the horn. "Be right there!" she shouted out the window.

As the two lovebirds drove off, I untangled my scarf and tied it over my head, taking in her advice and deciding to walk home.

Soaking in the summer's last downpour felt liberating, even though my soul felt betrayed. You never forget your first kiss or what you thought would become your forever love. I'd had his picture underneath my pillow for weeks, tarnished by my tears. When I returned home, the first step was shredding it—and the next was throwing it in the trash.

Geraldine married Richard many years later. At first, they were the hallmark of true love, but after several children, Geraldine fought depression and alcoholism. Their marriage eventually ended in divorce, leaving Richard a broken man.

Love's desire burns freely, and the person you choose will either lift you up or tear you down. When you trace your life in fine ink, your mind becomes adorned with woven memories like gossamer thread. One moment your heart is unstoppable—the next it's despondent, but eventually, it tries to awaken again. That's what young love is all about.

• • •

1946

Back at home, between washing our household laundry and wiping the peanut butter stains from the dishes, I heard Cora's tires squeal up the driveway. The tire marks were evidence that she and Smokey had been at it again.

I took the last bit of laundry off the clothesline, then headed back inside. But Cora grabbed the laundry basket out of my hands and threw it to the floor.

"Jane! Don't ignore me!" Her eyes were glued to mine.

"What's the matter with you?" I kneeled to pick up the clean laundry. "I'm the one doing everyone's chores around here. I don't see Smokey helping. He's always mooching off your paycheck!"

Cora slammed the door behind us. "Take that back or you can live someplace else! All you ever do is test me, Jane!" She poured a glass of wine, senselessly washing it back. "I know you've never approved of Smokey, but it's my house. And if you don't like things, you can get the hell out!"

Her countenance caved when she saw me throw the clean clothes back on the floor.

"Don't worry, Mother, you've made that very clear my entire life."

"Jane! If you ever get pregnant, I'll throw you both out!" She stood there, festering in her misery.

Moments later, I kicked open the front door with a pillow sack over my back, carrying my belongings like a refugee as I headed for the streets. The late afternoon sun struck my forehead while I fought my way into town, dodging traffic horns. The chaos surrounded me, growing thicker and louder. Sights and smells filled me until I couldn't stand any more.

"Get out of the way!" a man shouted as he turned the corner, barely missing me. I gave him the bird.

But just then, in lieu of my anger I saw my father about to turn the corner.

"Father!" I shouted. "Father, wait!"

When I caught up to him, I could see the years written all over his face. He looked exhausted and still wore the same shoes and torn jeans Mum had bought him.

I panted, barely able to catch my breath.

"Hello, Jane." He squinted, the sunlight in his eyes, trying to appear distracted. But his façade couldn't spare him this time. For once, I had outgrown his childishness.

"Father, why do you always push me away?" I followed him over to a street bench. "Do you even care about us?" I noticed his right eye twitching, probably from the uncomfortable conversation.

He sat back, looking at the crowds of pedestrians as the city's wastewater rushed into the gutters behind us. He was a man of few words. Paying us off was emotion enough, and showing feelings was rare—unless he was drinking. His deep forehead lines strained as he scratched his face and swatted at the flies.

I could sense he had fought for years to numb the guilt, but I was offering an olive branch for him to make amends. He just had to choose it.

"Jane, you wouldn't understand," he finally said while entertaining the pigeons that were pecking around the trash.

"Understand what?" I let my voice trail off a bit after that, afraid to hear what he had to say.

Father's discreetness was the death of my patience. What would be his alibi this time?

"Chuck isn't your brother." He cleared his throat. "He's not my biological son, Jane." His fleshy palms pushed into the sockets of his eyes.

The shock likened to tears streaming down my face—memories rinsed down a gutter.

"Why didn't anyone tell me this?" My mind retracted. "You had every opportunity, and you didn't think I was worth it!"

My anger had no limits.

He looked me in the eye, but it was subtle. "I didn't know how to tell you. Your mother and I were young and foolish."

Father paused, capsized by his sudden honesty.

"I'm sorry." He took a cigarette from his pocket and lit it, obviously needing to ground himself.

"So, that explains everything. I shook my head in disbelief. "Because you decided to keep this secret, I took the wrath for everyone."

Father reached to touch my shoulder, but all I could return was a blank stare. The case had been closed to discussion, and I took off to seek revenge back home.

"Jane, please!" Father's voice trailed from behind. "Don't do this!"

But I couldn't help but run. Faster and faster, I charged on until my limbs felt like engine blades. The skeletons were out, conjoined by my childhood nightmares. It was almost dinnertime, and Cora and Chuck were about to feel the fury I had masked for years.

Upon entering, I eyed the vase on the kitchen table and catapulted it at the wall to get their attention. Startled, both Chuck and Cora raced towards the living room.

"Don't either of you say a word! You all knew, and nobody told me." My soles dug into the glass shards as I braced to contain my dignity. "The truth is out now, so there's nothing to hide!" I said turning toward Cora's discombobulated frown. "Why didn't you tell me Chuck isn't my biological brother?"

Mum's face froze.

"I'm guessing your father told you that."

"He told me everything when I was in town today. You're all liars!" I shot a glance at Chuck trying to fade into the background.

"Now I know why you hate me! You're not my brother! You're a bastard!" I lunged at him, violently swinging my arms.

"Don't, Jane!" Cora intervened, ripping me from his collar.

Chuck refrained from fighting back, and his cruel eyes filled up with something I'd never seen before: tears.

"Don't protect him! Protect me!" I screamed as I attempted to break loose from Mum's grasp. But she didn't budge. Instead, she contained me like a wild animal.

In that moment I realized the bridge of communication was cut off, leaving me isolated.

"You both make me sick."

That evening I stayed at Geraldine's, but hiding from them didn't help the wounds. It didn't erase my brokenness or the damage that knowing the truth caused. I might as well have joined my brother. The only bastard left was me.

Chapter 6

WAR TIME IN AMERICA

Geraldine whispered, "Your mother is at the door."

She lifted the blinds to peek outside. "Think she wants to talk to you."

I rubbed my eyes and blinked a few times to refocus. "Tell her I'll be out in a minute."

Lifting my legs over the bed, I let out a yawn and stretched. Although the savory smell of scrambled eggs and bacon was enticing, I lost my appetite once I remembered Cora was waiting for me.

She looked discontent when I greeted her, the line between her brows deeper than before as if she were carrying a load of guilt.

"How've you been?"

"OK, I guess."

"I can't blame you for having a sharp tongue."

"Well, I learned from the best," I said, turning to walk back inside.

"It was never the right time, Jane." She looked away, searching for sympathy.

Repulsed by her ignorance, I lashed back.

"The right time would have been yesterday, or the day before that!" I said, trying to lower my voice. "Chuck hated me for your mistake, and I hope you live with that!"

"When you're ready to come home, the door's always open."

Cora had run out of excuses, and after she had a dose of her own medicine, something in her changed. Chuck never touched me after that. The secret had dissolved the abuse, but it still left the scars.

• • •

Across the bridge, the two rivers of the Youghiogheny and Monongahela rivaled each other like two jealous sisters without boundaries. It's where my next journey began: 729 May Street.

It felt like a whole new city within a city. I ran up the wooden steps to the second floor and smelled the fresh paint with a new perspective on life. Cora set the last box on the table and shrugged as she eyed the dust settling around the window frames. Smokey, on the other hand, headed toward her, a hungry savage. But Cora pushed him aside like a used shoe box and continued to organize the fridge.

That evening, after supper, Mum told me about a close call she'd had on the road. Her hide was thicker than most animals', and she wasn't afraid to fight ugly.

"Last night, I was attacked by a man who didn't want to pay his taxi fare," Cora said, wiping the crumbs from the table.

"What did you do?" I leaned forward overcome with disbelief.

"Well, I reached back and pulled the knife out of his hands, and he fled before I could garnish his wallet.

Cora disregarded her dangerous encounter like a walk in the park. Her job was scary alright; weekly newspapers reported men getting shot in the back of the head just for opening their doors. But for Cora, these events were just as everyday as women getting perms. If it meant keeping a roof over our heads, she'd do almost anything.

"Did you call the police?" I gulped and shoved the last piece of pie in my mouth. She passed me a napkin and grinned.

"When problems arise, Jane, you've got to deal with them. The cops are pigs. They'll find you guilty in a man's world, handcuff you, and whisk you away to jail. Defend yourself, but keep your mouth shut!"

That evening, I admired her rough edges. Learning how to deal with problems was just the start of how I learned to survive the streets. After supper, I got busy emptying the last of our moving boxes. As fate would have it, I found a locket with a picture of Cora and my father inside. It rested in my palms as I looked down at the broken glass, saddened that the two young lovers in the photo were unaware of their future demise.

My musings were cut short. I heard Mum's footsteps coming up the hallway, so I hid the locket under the mattress. The sweet trail of her perfume followed, and she leaned forward to kiss me goodnight.

Beyond the window glass, I could see my reflection looking back at me. And an identical outline of a little girl appeared as a fearless survivor. She was my hero.

• • •

It was 1951, and the United States drafted thousands of men into service, including my mother's first cousin JR, with whom she was incredibly close. Chuck was also drafted and stationed in Germany.

He and I were never the same after I learned the news from Father. It didn't bring us together, only further apart. But I still saluted him when he waved goodbye to serve our country. Strangely, I felt as if I were drafted into the war with him. He felt like the enemy I didn't want to hate, but we stood on opposite lines.

It was during those times I'd find Mum praying by herself late at night, but she never knew I was watching. The war changed our households one layer at a time. Newspaper tabloids told the stories of deceased soldiers, writing unthinkable horrors into our imaginations. The wounded had come home in caskets, a harsh picture of America after war. We were granted freedom out of sacrifice.

I sympathized whenever she'd say she missed Chuck, and I placed my own feelings aside. But deep down, I wanted him to feel the fear I had felt, the panic he'd created inside me. When Chuck returned, his temper had amplified, and his melancholy disposition spoiled any chance of reconciliation.

Growing tired of all the negativity, I turned off the news.

"Why did you turn off the television?" Cora set down her glasses to give me the look.

"That's all we talk about anymore. There are other things to pay attention to," I said, pouring a glass of water.

"But that's what it is, Jane. A war. It doesn't just suddenly stop or disappear."

I drank down the cool water, eliminating the sour taste in my mouth. "I'm going outside."

The world was shifting, and so was I. My mind would sense things before they occurred, but I ignored it. Superstitions weren't a popular viewpoint, and if you had a prediction, you were called a liar. Was it my active imagination—or was it a gift?

• • •

It was my senior year of high school. Fall was around the corner, and the leaves were turning colors. My favorite part was the pine needles. They smelled invigorating, but I could sense more was on the horizon than just the changing of seasons.

The older I became, the more vivid my dreams and visions were. I borrowed books from the school library to seek answers, but I was uncomfortable in seeking the truth. Some people called it hocus-pocus, but I called it my sixth sense.

Everything started subtly, but one day, my dreams became hostile. It was 1952. The war had become the focus of the world, and my dreams turned into premonitions.

Surrounded by a ring of lights, I watched an angelic tide of white shrouds move to ethereal energy. My body wasn't coherent enough to wake. Instead, I was entombed, barely able to move. It was as if a projector screen were showing me glimpses of the future.

"Watch out for July!" A high-octane, disembodied voice echoed, shattering my eardrums like explosives.

A bomb ruptured into a sea of dew. It expanded like a rubber band but didn't fade. Peering into molten lava, I saw an image of myself wearing a white cap and gown. The voice grew louder, splintering my lungs into tiny fragments. Fire was melting away my flesh like pasta strands.

Pandemonium set in as I struggled to breathe. "Watch out for July!" The voice roared through the meridians of my body. Soldiers were scattered everywhere.

Gasping for air, I awoke in a cold sweat, screaming violently. "July! Something horrible is going to happen in July!"

Disoriented, I kicked off the sheets and was inconsolable. Bewildered, Mum raced to get warm milk and a washcloth.

"It was just a dream, Jane." She patted my forehead. "They always feel real, but they're only nightmares."

Somewhere between wakefulness and sleep, I continued to resist.

"No, this was different. I heard them clearly," I professed, continuing to pinch myself.

"Who are they?" Mum was troubled by my lack of coherency.

"Something tragic will happen soon—I just don't know what it is. You've got to believe me!" I stared deep into her eyes.

But rather, Mum remained insistent I was only dreaming and switched the light off. "They're just nightmares, Jane. Nothing more."

• • •

I graduated that year in June, wearing my white cap and gown. The weather forecast was clear of storms, and only the pretty blue sky could be seen for miles. Mum couldn't resist documenting every moment up until graduation.

"OK, hold still," she insisted.

"Mum, really! You've already taken a dozen photos. We're going to be late!"

"Alright. Let me grab my purse." Her voice trailed behind.

Just then, the phone rang.

"I'll get it!" I shouted as I fixed my dress. "Hello?"

"Hello, Jane. This is your Uncle Thurman. Is your mother around?" His voice sounded frantic.

Uncle Thurman was Mum's half-brother, a religious man devoted to his faith. They didn't speak often, so having an unexpected call must have meant something important.

"She'll be back in a moment; she's collecting her things. Today's my—"

"JR was killed overseas. Please tell your mother. I can't talk right now."

Without reservation, I screamed, and the phone slipped from my hands.

"What is it, Jane?" Mum rushed over and shook me like a rag doll. "Jane! Jane, what is it? Tell me, goddammit!"

"JR. He was killed." I whimpered softly. Mum collapsed onto the kitchen floor in a flood of agony as I kneeled below to comfort her.

That afternoon, I somberly joined the lineup of my classmates. I felt death before I could feel happiness.

JR had just turned twenty-one. His body was returned to us in July after they located his limbs. The funeral parlor draped the American flag over the sealed mahogany coffin and covered it in flowers. JR's services were a grim reminder of the perils of war and the courage it takes to defend our country.

Shortly afterward, his mother died of a stroke. But the worst feeling was knowing I had dreamt about it. Mum was wrong. They weren't all just nightmares.

• • •

After graduation, I began to trust my intuition, but I kept my thoughts disciplined. It was my only way of feeling normal. Life, somehow had to move on.

In the meantime, escaping the preconceived notion I had manifested JR's death was the devil at my back and had disrupted my innocence. This sinful second guessing had me chasing God. But perhaps it was a gift from my higher consciousness. God didn't have time for coincidences. The Bible calls it divine providence.

Pondering my childhood, I celebrated that he had equipped me with a strong mind and strength. Clearly, God was in control of my story. Just like a complicated musical score, it took time, but I learned to create a masterpiece from the lessons, and I grew thick skin. God was in the wilderness, not just in the church.

Riding up Stone Alley to the Versailles Cemetery, life and death rippled onward, as effortlessly as the seasons changed. It didn't alarm me any. In fact, the cemetery became a place for solitude and hours of thinking.

Often, a deep yawn would creep up on me, and I'd doze off against the headstones, making way for inspiring visions and daydreams. The spiritual world was an abundant resource there, where I learned to harness my abilities. I was just seventeen.

Chapter 7

PUPPETS ON A STRING

Living through the 1950s meant using your wits, especially as a young woman. You needed to know how to pick your battles, what the latest fashion was, and whom to marry. If you mastered those things, you were golden. Imagine it—those were some of the "headaches" that kept us awake at night. What society fed you, what the commercials promised, and what your girlfriends swore was the truth had the weight of the world on your shoulders.

We were puppets on a string, trying to break free from the rules that were customary of young women. I could finally say I was old enough to make my own choices, so I had to plan tactfully. The only problem was being a notorious loudmouth, so if anything got the best of me, that was my downfall.

• • •

Cora had it set in stone that everyone who was religious was a Bible-preaching nut. She schooled me on the different religions and criticized the self-serving pastors who'd suck the lives from people's pockets.

Even though she couldn't stand any of them, I assumed the only way back to Jesus was going to church. So, one Sunday, I convinced her to take me. Her sister Birdy was the epitome of a Bible do-gooder. In fact, people crowned my aunt the *Queen of the Word* because she knew the Bible from top to bottom. However, she had her imperfections like anyone—she babbled too fast and spit like a camel when she thought no one was looking. Cora and Birdy only talked during the holidays, but she was adamant about sending us *Come just as you are* invitations.

"Come on, Jane, we're going to be late!" Cora yelled from inside the car.

"OK, OK! Just give me one more second!" I was busy trying to line my upper lip. The engine horn was still honking as I scampered to straighten my skirt.

"Hold on a sec!" I wobbled on my heels, tugging at the car door. There we were riding toward God's paradise—into the heartland of religious customs.

"Am I dressed appropriately?" I asked as we pulled up to the church's graveled entrance, noticing an assembly of simply clad pedestrians holding Bibles. My brightly colored polka-dot dress stood out.

"Well, you wanted to come. I'm dropping you off right here." Cora pulled her sunglasses down to look at the women covered from head to foot.

"Jesus accepts everyone," I huffed, slamming the door loudly. "Call you when I'm done!" I waved.

Cora caught sight of Birdy and rolled her eyes at me, then quickly drove off.

I'll admit, I found myself a little overdressed walking up to Sunday service. Everyone was dressed conservatively and without a speck of makeup. "What did you get yourself into this time, Jane?" I blushed sheepishly.

"Jane! Is that you?"

"Oh, hi, Aunt Birdy." My voice lifted as I ignored all the stares. Birdy's pretty, black hair was neatly in place—not to mention her thin eyebrows arched to perfection and her stunning heart-shaped lips. She frequently was mistaken for Rosalind Russell.

"Oh, honey! You can't take communion today!" She looked at me in horror. "You're wearing lipstick and nail polish," she whispered, nudging me away from the church entrance.

"Well, I didn't know." I cowered, trying to cover myself up with a scarf.

"Oh, no, no, no. Have you been born again? Your mother lied to me, didn't she?" Her brows frowned with dissatisfaction like I had committed a cardinal sin.

"What is 'born again'? I am born, Birdy!" My silly grin turned upside down.

"Jane, you can't join us today," she said, turning around to spit.

"I'm alive, aren't I?" I grinned with displeasure.

"No! Born again to Jesus!" She looked irritated, grabbing me by the arm to quiet me down. "You'll need to be baptized first. And you definitely can't wear polka dots!"

At that point, I wasn't sure if I was at a charade party or an occult parade. "Oh, the hell with it! You can all kiss my ass!"

Birdy's mouth dropped open like a gumball machine. "Jane, the Lord is listening!"

"To my words? What about your words, you camel-spitting bigot! You're all crazy—every one of you! Why didn't you tell me God prefers non-makeup-wearing sinners?"

I marched to the edge of the parking lot. Birdy stood paralyzed in disbelief, along with the entire congregation.

"Don't worry, I'll make it easy for everyone." And that's when I removed the scarf from around my shoulders, showing off my skin in broad daylight.

They all gasped.

"I'd rather be out here than inside with a bunch of you jerks!"

· · ·

Cursing the entire way home, I swung open our front door and headed to get my skates.

"What happened? Is Birdy a Bible bully?" Cora chuckled.

"Not funny." I tried not to smile. "How can people be so narrow-minded, Mum? Is wearing lipstick and nail polish really a holy sin?"

"Chin up, girl. It's not all that bad. At least you don't spit like a camel." Her devilish smile cracked, causing us both to break into a belly laugh.

"Well, at least I'm not a puppet on a string," I said, lacing up.

· · ·

Fall was drawing near, and that meant Pennsylvania's pallet was changing to colors of bright oranges and yellows. Whisking along, I bulldozed through the pastures, hearing the crackle and pop of twigs once again. As summer had finally come to an end, I wouldn't miss the pesky mosquitoes, but I would miss my freedom.

It was time for me to get a job, and the dreaded nine-to-five Mum talked about had me wishing I was a kid again: The American workforce was hungry for young blood, just like the mosquitoes buzzing at our doorstep.

"All employers are like snakes. They don't care about your resume—they just want your undergarments." Mum shoveled the trash into a garbage bag defiantly.

Boy, I'd hate to say she was right, but within a year, I had gone through jobs like chewing gum. At my first job—a housekeeper—I worked until I almost broke my neck. I slipped on a wet floor of soap suds and took a tumble down a flight of stairs.

My second job was as a delivery girl, handing takeout orders through car windows. But that didn't work out either because too many men wanted to take me for a ride.

And my third job—a cashier at a nearby movie theater—was another disaster. I worked for peanuts, which barely bought me popcorn.

Jobs were like pit stops back then; only worse was the unequal pay for women. I made an hourly wage below the poverty line. Still, it was up to me to look for an apartment to show Mum I could be independent. And it couldn't have come any sooner. Cora was busy having it out with Smokey after hearing rumors of his infidelity.

Smokey pounded on the bedroom door with his knuckles. "Cora, open the door, sweetheart. You know I wouldn't cheat on you!" He pressed his forehead against the door frame, clenching a handful of fresh roses.

She abruptly opened the door, causing him to stumble forward. "What's this, then?" She smacked his face with a dress coat covered in red lipstick. "I don't wear red lipstick. Do you wear red lipstick?"

"For God's sake, Cora, I don't know where this came from!"

"I want your things out of here tonight!" She stomped past him, slamming the door in his face.

I watched my childhood replay, like a slow depression, until I decided to take matters into my own hands.

One by one, Cora threw his suits out the bedroom door. I entered, bobbing and weaving around the chaos.

"Hold on, you guys! Listen to me for a second. Smokey, what Cora is trying to say is that she wants commitment. So why don't you man up and marry her?" I smacked his forearm.

"What on earth are you doing, Jane?" She scowled as she brushed back a few strands of hair from her face and straightened her posture.

"I'm doing what you should have done years ago!"

Everything in me wanted to run Smokey out of our lives, but I knew Cora couldn't live without him.

"Just marry her, will you?" I said, throwing a tie around his neck.

Both of them stood in dismay like a math equation had been solved and the holy grail extracted from the anus of Mother Nature.

"Grow up!" I said before leaving the room satisfied.

But my schooling backfired. Cora would continue to suspect Smokey of cheating. He was from the alpha breed—handsome and cocky without apology—and she couldn't look past it.

Smokey tried to live up to Cora's standards, but everyone who knew him knew he wasn't the marrying type. So, Mum did what she did best, which was to search him from top to bottom every time he'd come home. She even went so far as to monitor his car mileage.

Sure, I knew he was cheating, but he was clever as a chimpanzee.

● ● ●

Using earplugs to drown out their arguing, I searched the morning paper. As I skimmed over the local jobs, I happened across one that seemed perfect for me.

A bookkeeper for a beer dispensary. It sounded enticing. Cautiously, I sipped my morning coffee, trying not to burn my tongue and reading over the job description. It only took a phone call, and before I could count to ten, I was rushing to the interview, reciting my speech.

"I got the job!" I triumphed as I walked through the door later that afternoon, only to find dirty dishes in the sink. No one was home to help me celebrate, but despite being disappointed, I felt liberated. The only thing left to do was find an apartment.

After touring a handful of low-income rentals, I set my heart on a small studio. My savings just barely made the first month's rent, but the landlord handed over the keys and wished me luck as she puffed cigarette smoke in my face.

"I wonder what Mum will think?" I hesitated, realizing my impulsiveness had gotten the best of me. Either way, I was old enough to make my own decisions, but I couldn't shake the feeling she'd crucify me for it.

"When were you planning on telling me?" Mum's stare had me naked in doubt.

"I was going to tell you, but I was scared you'd talk me out of it."

She started ripping out magazine ads with a jerk. "Don't come knocking when you need money." She sank back into the chair and threw up her feet.

"You'll never miss me, anyway," I said, grabbing the last of my belongings.

• • •

After moving in what few boxes I could carry, the tiny apartment was as bare as boncs. I hadn't a clue you needed so much just to fill a tiny space. So, the next morning I headed to the local furniture store to purchase something to sleep on.

"May I help you, miss?" A scruffy-faced man greeted me.

"Yes. In fact, I would like to purchase a couch." I looked around with a demure grin, trying to remain composed.

"Well, you've come to the right place. We have some beautiful pieces to choose from. Some are priced higher than others of course, but have a look around. Do you have a preference?" He poked his nose over my purse, sniffing around for money.

"Well, not particularly." My eyes filled with optimism as I hunted around. "Oh! I like that piece over there!" I spotted a beautiful floral print loveseat and headed over to feel the cushions.

"Oh, that one? What an excellent choice. However, it's probably out of your price range."

"I beg your pardon?" I plunked down on the sofa and looked at him crossly.

"Well, a lady like you. Forgive me," he corrected himself. "May I ask where your husband is? Perhaps he could help you pay for it?"

"Husband?" I leaped to my feet.

"Yes. Your husband?" He scratched his chin confused.

"You son of a bitch, I don't need a husband!"

"Excuse me, ma'am, please lower your voice."

"Well, pardon me. I didn't think you had to be married to be treated with respect around here!"

• • •

After a rough night's sleep on the floor with some blankets and pillows, the confrontation with the creep from the furniture store gave me enough ammo to get my hands dirty and work overtime to pay for a couch. One particular day, I arrived early at the dispensary and noticed we had an overstock of product. The mildew coming from the run-down building left me sickly—it agitated my nostrils. Add to that, the musky heat, the flies buzzing around and landing on my sweat, and my boss acting like a rude old goat—there was nothing glamourous about it at all.

There I was in a hellhole of mixed proportions, organizing a landfill of bottles.

"Keep them organized! If not, you'll have to redo the entire order tomorrow," my boss bleated as he dozed off behind his command center.

Carefully, I started to reach for a bottle in the corner of the shelf when I heard a soft squeaking. But unalarmed, I continued to mark the inventory.

"There it goes again," I whispered. Curious, I peeked behind a row of dusty bottles, and there it was—a gigantic, hideous rat! Its eyes intensified and festered with fire as it chomped on dry bones. When it saw me, its fur stood up like spikes. We both shrieked at the top of our lungs.

"Ahh!" I screamed, running like a wild horse out the gate.

"What in God's name is going on?" My boss awoke in a panic, knocking over his lunch.

"A rat! A huge fat rat!" I threw off my upper garments, feeling like the critter was all over me.

My boss appeared amused but rushed to my defense. "Jane, you can't leave now—I need you!" He grabbed a broom from the side of the door.

"Nope. Sorry. You've got the wrong girl!" I kept running, practically pulling out my hair.

I could hear his voice echo as I got farther away. "Jane, please, I'll kill it!"

"No way! I'll be back for my check next week!" I hollered.

By the time I reached my doorstep, I was exasperated. You wouldn't believe it, but for a long time after that, I slept with a kitchen knife under my pillow and mouse traps around my bed.

• • •

Discouraged about finding another job, I went outside to catch some fresh air before taking a brisk walk.

Underneath the umbrella of currency, the world carried on without me. I was just like that fat rodent. We both fended for ourselves and needed a roof over our heads. We were rebels without a cause, rummaging through trash that others had left behind.

Moments later, I started to cross the street without noticing an oncoming vehicle. The driver held down the horn and pumped the brakes, missing me by a sliver. "Get out of the road! Don't you look where you're going?"

As I regained my composure and shooed away the smoke, I noticed an old woman signaling for me to come over.

"Come. Come!" She swiftly gestured.

Mum had warned me about traveling strangers, but there was something intriguing by the way she lured me in. Bizarrely, the mysterious woman and her caravan seemed to have appeared out of thin air.

Immediately I noticed her coarse skin was aged by the sun, and her wiry hair was like dry thistles. The elderly woman's jawline was pronounced with a pointed chin, and an amulet hung halfway down her neck.

"What are you running from?" She peered deep into my eyes, hypnotizing my pupils.

"Running? I'm not running from anything." I picked nervously at my dress.

"You have a powerful mind and a willful heart." She grabbed my hands, studying every line. "Aha! That explains it!" She focused for a moment. "You're on the cusp of Virgo and Libra." She smoothed over my palms, scanning deeper. "Your mother will remarry soon. And you'll marry twice. But! Beware of a light-haired woman who will come into your life—she is treacherous! Keep away from her!" The traveler firmly gripped my wrists. "She's dangerous."

"I'll be careful," I assured her, removing my wrists from her grasp.

"My dear, you've got an immeasurable amount of strength, but there are darker days ahead of you."

I steadied my gaze, so as not to appear too eager to know the details.

"Well, I don't know what to do," I admitted, feeling defeated at every turn.

"You should be on stage. You'd make a wonderful actress. But something tells me you're being held back by someone."

It was as if she knew me and all my internal thoughts, but as abruptly as she came into my life, I had to end our conversation. Mum would kill me if I wasn't on time for dinner.

"I have to get going. It's getting late." I thanked her. The sunset was proceeding behind the mountain range, but when I turned back to wave good-bye, she had already vanished.

The long walk home had me searching for answers, trying to bend reason with time. Gypsy magic had abducted me, as I rinsed off my face before supper. Was she just a figment of my imagination?

Although I never encountered her again, she'd laid a footprint in my soul that would haunt me in the future. Her premonitions would bear fruit.

• • •

The very next week, Cora called me enthused to share to news.

"Jane, you'll never believe it!" Her voice sounded energized.

"What is it?"

"Smokey proposed!"

I could feel my appetite deteriorate.

"That's wonderful," I said meekly.

After I hung up, my memories resurfaced. The old woman had prophesized right. We're not always aware of our destiny. Whether for richer or poorer or running from rodents, we can't escape the hands of the universe. This was just the start.

"Just for tonight, I'll slip into bed, one last time surrounded by mousetraps, and giggle at my own insanity," I thought.

Chapter 8

HEARTS OF MEN - PART I

In 1954, Cora and Smokey finally married, and I returned home.

My living in the center of town in a rat-infested apartment just wasn't cutting it but neither was living under their roof. I felt like an inconvenience.

The winter leaves were covered in white now, and the bone-chilling cold became a stale reminder of the past. The air was relentless and fussy, burning my nose and turning my cheeks a rosy red. I hustled to keep busy and found work at a nearby movie theater, selling tickets.

Inside, the warmth of the old theater smelled of enchanted oak, and the fine fabrics that flowed to the floor made it timeless. I could hear the whistling of the wind battering the old window frames at midday, and when the theater was quiet, I could sneak in and watch old movies, pretending to be the actress I always wanted to be.

Each character mirrored my internal desires of whom I wished to become—someone who gambled on life and lived by her own rules, not living by someone else's standards, and hovering above the peaks and valleys of my heart.

The flickering of aged films hypnotized me as the credits rolled by. I was mesmerized by its language and the fantasies it played out. But in my twenty-year-old heart, I was searching for so much more, something deeper than the actor's clever smile. The hearts of men were plenty, but no one spoke to my heart as easily anymore. Maybe my strength and independence were a curse like Rapunzel cast away in a tower. Or perhaps I was just unattainable because of my past.

"Jane, you need a life. All you do is work, work, work!" my girlfriend Thelma whined over the phone. "Just put yourself together, and I'll be there in an hour to pick you up." Her voice fluttered like the wings of sparrows.

"Alright, just give me some time, will ya?" I set the phone down, struggling to take off my shoes.

The bathroom mirror forced me to see my youthfulness. I twisted the lipstick wand upward, pressing it onto my full lips and smiling with confidence. The mascara bristles carefully brushed each lash, activating my green eyes, before I applied the last stroke of rouge across my cheekbones. Each moment was a process. It took a steady hand and an artist's eye to make sure I didn't leave lines in my foundation. But the most satisfying part was slipping on my dress. It fit perfectly over my curves without an inch to spare. However, it wouldn't have been complete without my heels. And, as I placed the last bobby pin in my hair, the makeover was finished. I sprayed on Mum's perfume in even strokes, then grabbed my winter coat and waited anxiously for my ride.

Soon enough, I heard Thelma's horn honking up a storm. Her blaring car radio irritated Cora, to say the least. I shuffled one last time to get my purse in order and tugged at my dress to keep it in place. The icy chill took my breath away as I opened the door and raced to the passenger door for shelter. Once inside, Thelma cranked up the radio even louder. We peeled out of the driveway like two wild hearts set free. It was an adrenaline rush, the time of our lives.

The music hall wasn't far from home. Once we entered, we were the life of the party. Dancing through the crowd of young men and women, I became lost in its abyss.

"Hey! There's my friend John!" Thelma shouted into my ear.

"I can't hear you!" I shouted back as I carried on dancing to the music.

"John! He's a close friend of mine. I'll be right back!"

But before I could drift deeper into the sound, I was being pulled by the arm.

"Jane, meet John!" Thelma spun me around.

Instantly, I felt a connection. His eyes were hauntingly familiar, igniting something inside me that I'd never known before. I had a deep desire to be in his presence. I'll never forget his handshake and the energy I felt touching his skin. The universe was up to no good, but the dose of poison felt invigorating the closer we became. It was as if it were only the two of us and the music, a magnetism of wizardry that fused my soul to his. We stared into each other's eyes, like twin flames handpicked from the universe. I felt overcome by our chemistry and fell madly in love when he took me in his arms.

John gently placed my hands on his chest, and I could feel his heartbeat. Our chemistry invoked danger because we both knew we were as fragile as glass.

But he didn't shy away. He held my body securely and touched the sides of my face as if he knew me more than I knew myself. Then all at once, he leaned in and kissed me softly. As I surrendered, he pulled me closer, running his hands down the back of my dress and up the sides of my body until the intensity and passion were interrupted.

"Jane, it's getting late." Thelma nudged me. "I see you've met John?" she smirked with sarcasm. "You'll have to excuse us, but we have to get going. Here's her number." She handed him a piece of paper and led me toward the exit.

"Goodnight, John." I smiled.

That evening, I couldn't sleep. I tossed and turned, replaying our fated meeting.

"Looks like you've met someone," Cora said casually as she scooped bacon onto my breakfast plate.

"What makes you think that?" I yawned letting out a sweet sigh.

"You've just walked to the fridge twice and didn't grab anything. And you're smiling like you've met Prince Charming. So ... who is he?"

"No one. Well, someone. I don't know, he's just ... amazing."

She poured us some juice while studying my expression.

"Jane, I hope you're careful with this man. It sounds like lust to me."

"Oh, Mum, really. I know what I felt!"

But she wasn't impressed. She whisked the eggs like she wanted to start a fire.

The phone rang, and we both rushed to grab it at the same time.

"I'll get it!" I ran, practically breaking my leg over a wedge sticking out of the floor. "Hello?"

Anxiously awaiting John's voice, I heard Thelma's instead.

"Well, that was some kiss last night!"

"Oh, Thelma! You got my heart tied up in knots! I thought you were him!" I said, practically scolding her.

"I can be if you like," she said in a deep voice.

"You jerk!"

"Don't worry. I spoke to him earlier, and he said he'd call you."

"Thanks, Thelma."

"For what?"

"Well, for introducing us. For whatever it's worth, I didn't think I would be on a blind date, let alone become completely infatuated with a guy I've barely talked to." I blushed.

"Well, you've got to let me know what happens."

"I will."

That afternoon I was going stir-crazy, waiting for John's call. I'd practically given up, but that evening, just as dinner was being served, the phone rang. Cora and Smokey glared at me as if I were a salesman interrupting dinner time.

"I'll get it!" I said, tossing my napkin midair.

"Hello," I said, praying that it wasn't Thelma.

"Can I speak to Jane?" John's voice took me by surprise.

"This is Jane." My heart thumped out of my chest.

"I'd like to see you again. Can I pick you up tonight?" He patiently waited while I figured out how to hide my response from Mother.

"That would be fine. How about eight o'clock?" I whispered the address.

"Great. Look for me in a black Chevy—I'll be parked out front."

"Alright, see you soon."

"Who was that?" Cora was quick to ask.

"Oh, uh, that was just Thelma." I turned to excuse myself from the table. "I'll be going out with her this evening."

"Alright, well, have a nice time." Mum looked unconvinced.

She always seemed to know when I was keeping something from her. But I pretended otherwise, sneaking away like a lioness into my den.

• • •

I raced to my bedroom, panicking over what to wear. Finally, after demolishing my entire closet, I found my favorite trousers and threw on a floral blouse. Hopping on one leg to the bathroom, I slipped on my heels and doused myself with perfume. Come to think of it, I must have smelled like the Garden of Eden.

Time was ticking, and before I knew it, it was eight. Shoveling my makeup into my handbag, I took one last look in the mirror. Anticipating

John's arrival, my eyes were glued to the vehicles coming up the street, but I had yet to spot the black Chevy.

Outside, winter had shown no peace while the snow fairies covered the landscape. But even with the cold, my heart glowed with fantasy once I saw his high beams coming from around the corner.

Without time to spare, I calmed my nerves and assumed my alter ego as Katharine Hepburn, then gracefully approached his car. John hopped out and opened the side door. He wore relaxed jeans and a dark leather coat that smelled brand new. As I slipped into the car seat, he leaned over to fasten the belt across my lap and stopped to stare into my eyes with a seductive smile before we drove into the dark night.

On the outskirts of town, the stars shone brighter than ever, and the city below looked like ice castles. We pulled up to a tiny motel where the vacancy sign was barely legible. Youth can never be taken for granted. We were young and driven by mad desire, clinging to eternity with nothing to hold us back.

John's eyes were aroused as he carried me inside the motel room and laid me on the soft linen.

"Are you sure?" he asked, leaning over to kiss me softly.

"I'm sure." I touched his handsome jawline and ran my fingers through his hair. It was my first experience making love, and I wanted it to be perfect.

Taking the lead, he removed his shirt, allowing my shyness to fade as we removed each other's clothing. The sexual intensity was like a drug. I wanted to savor every moment like it was our last.

He tilted me back and ran his hands down my body like I was a piece of fine sculpture. My body arched with pleasure as his hands and lips aroused me. We moved effortlessly with the endurance of angels— no place was as heavenly as this. The bed frame shook as John entered me, a powerful sensation that was forbidden. His hair sailed over my breasts as he kissed me without boundaries, and our bodies became one. I could feel every part that made us uniquely human. He moaned softly as I sailed on top of him. That's when I cried out his name. Digging my nails into his shoulders, I collapsed over his body and shivered with ecstasy.

After our lovemaking, we stared into each other's eyes. I lay in his embrace, looking up at the ceiling of the motel room in nakedness. We would make love a few more times that evening, and when the morning sun lifted its sleepy eyes, we fell deeper for one another. As we gathered our clothes that were scattered around the room, I couldn't help but feel different.

The early dawn was still awakening as he dropped me off. I blew him a kiss goodbye before closing the door and tiptoeing inside. Womanhood had finally come and sealed a kiss that would haunt me forever.

From that moment forward, every chance we had, we spent together. The world was at our fingertips. Maybe I was a sinner for not waiting until marriage—or maybe young hearts just can't help but be free.

• • •

"This boy you're dating, what does he do?" Cora's body tensed as she perched herself in my bedroom doorway.

"He works at the mill yard."

"You're going to need to settle down with someone who can provide for you, Jane. You understand that, don't you?" She countered my defiance with a glare.

"I know, Mum, but we haven't talked about that yet. We just like being together." I started to hum tenderly.

"Jane, look at me! Haven't you learned anything from my mistakes? You need to find yourself a decent man. Someone who will give you the world." She seemed to be fighting her own heart.

"I'm not like you. And besides, it's too late—I'm in love with him."

"Well, don't come to me if you end up alone and pregnant!"

"Fine with me!" I said, slamming the bathroom door.

That evening, John and I hung out at the theater as we always did, but I could tell something was troubling him.

"What's on your mind? You haven't said a word to me tonight."

"Nothing." John hesitated like he was trying to hold himself together.

"I can tell something is bothering you. Look at me, will you?"

He cowered away but then finally said what I feared. "I have to go away for a few months."

The news ruptured my heart.

"When were you going to tell me?" I stood up, brushing my composure to the floor.

"I have to leave by the end of next week." John paused. "I have to, Jane—my father runs the operation, and I have to go!"

"Well, take me with you." My eyes searched for his comfort but got none.

"I can't." He lit a cigarette. "I'll be back before you know it. I promise."

"How could you do this?" I shoved his hand away. "Why couldn't you just be man enough to tell me and not leave it to the last minute?"

My anger unraveled, a cascade of emotions.

"The last thing I want is to leave you, but my old man has the final say."

"Well, I guess this is goodbye?"

"Jane, don't do this. If I didn't have to go, I wouldn't."

But the reality was ripping us apart. I felt our future vanish behind the curtains.

"A promise is just a promise, John, but will you still want me when you return?" I started walking out in the pouring rain, leaving him behind on the theatre doorsteps.

After he left town, I never stopped thinking of him. His kiss and pale-blue eyes would forever be the willow tree in my soul. I feel it even now, though it may sound crazy. Hearts of men live in a parallel universe with only two directions: love and heartbreak. But when a woman's universe falls apart, there is only hell.

Chapter 9

HEARTS OF MEN - PART 2

"I was twenty-one, and women didn't have many options back then.
Marriage was a milestone for a young woman.
If you were past the age of twenty, you were considered a spinster."

—JANE CORSARO

After my twenty-first birthday, I still hadn't heard from John. My heart ached for him, but life carried on. Working forty hours at a cosmetic counter distracted me some of the time.

The reality, though, was I'd become a zombie—like right out of a horror movie. An emotionless soul looking for human flesh … someone's heart I could break since mine was broken.

"Jane! Jane! Wake up, will you?" My co-worker Irma shook me out of a daydream. "Turn on the news! Is that your dad? It sure looks like him. The news is saying he just jumped into the Youghiogheny River. What is this world coming to?"

"Jumped?" I rushed over to the TV.

My father was a daredevil alright, adventurous as they come and bloody Irish to the marrow. There he was, making headlines, which I'm sure didn't bother him any. But what was worse was that the news continued to replay my father in his birthday suit for the entire world to see. Come to find out, he only jumped because of a dare—and because he wanted to cover his bar tab. Fish wasn't one to turn down a bet, so he did what any hothead would do: leap into the belly of the beast.

My cheeks turned fire red with embarrassment. That afternoon, I asked to be excused from the gossip swarming the makeup aisles. I needed a place to hide.

Cora, of course, never asked about John, although she knew I was in love with him. She just encouraged her objective of my finding a man with a large bank account. The sour patch in my mouth puckered at the thought because I couldn't imagine marrying someone I didn't love. I needed something more than a coffee-ground marriage full of heartache, revenge, or adultery. Tea and honey sounded more satisfying—It meant more to me to have a partner provide sweetness than woo me with money.

Thelma eventually got me to agree to going out again. I met my share of men, but no one compared to John.

"Excuse me, would you like to dance?" A puny voice tapped on my shoulder. I turned around to make eye contact with an awkwardly thin man wobbling on his feet to the music.

"Sure," I shrugged politely, as I tried to separate my feelings. We danced a few songs before I caught myself yawning and signaled to Thelma it was time to go.

"You're so beautiful." His starstruck eyes widened as he drew me in closer, trying to nuzzle a kiss.

"I apologize, but I have to get going. My mother has me on a curfew." My head dodged his in the nick of time, leaving him to kiss the air.

Thelma rushed to my defense and handed over my purse. "Have a nice evening—we're leaving now."

"Donald, my name is Donald." His voice cracked short.

"Goodnight, Don," I said, trying to race out the door.

My interest in him was pretty much nonexistent. His for me was undeniable. The next weekend, he'd made sure I danced only with him, shooing other suitors away like a billy goat puffing his tiny chest muscles.

Eventually, I caved in and allowed him to escort me home—after buying me a drink.

He projected a frail demeanor. His body was gangly with feminine features and a pitchy voice that cracked with a slight whine every time he got excited. I could only imagine the ridicule he must have endured growing up.

But Donald had something that most women would have died for: money. And lots of it. He would've given me the world. He was the man every mother adored, but I kept running in the opposite direction. That didn't faze him. He never gave up. Instead, he grew persistent and overtly obnoxious in his wooing. Sometimes he'd arrive unannounced at my doorstep, earning Cora's stamp of approval, then overstay his welcome.

• • •

"He's a delightful man, Jane. Look on the bright side—he could offer you a wonderful life."

"I need more than just security, Mum. I'd rather be with John."

"John?" She took a swig of beer and swallowed. "He'll only give you problems—don't you realize that? You can grow to love Donald." Her face eased of worry. "Open your heart a little. Donald has never given up on you. Where's John?" Her eyes squinted with intention.

"Well, what if I can't love him? Then what?"

"Well, then there's always divorce," she said sarcastically.

• • •

It was all a lot to think about, but every time I had a chance to think, Donald's persistent phone calls startled me mid-thought. He stalked me all summer, obsessing at the chance of a romantic relationship. When he wouldn't stop, some irrational goblin in my head told me to give him a chance.

I tried hard to push my feelings for John aside as I ignored Donald's foolish attempts to impress, which made me uncomfortable. His cologne didn't smell like John's. It smelled like fern trees. And he chewed his food like a mule.

One evening, after we pulled into my front driveway, I suddenly felt anxious, hardly able to breathe. That's when Donald leaned over to kiss me.

"Please, don't," I said before I could catch the words from escaping. "Please, Don, it's just too soon." I looked at him with melancholy eyes.

Visibly frustrated, he sunk like a slug back onto his side of the seat.

"I love you, Jane."

"I see… but I'm just not there yet. You've got to give me some more time."

He gripped the steering wheel and frowned. "Well, alright. I'll pick you up tomorrow?"

"Let's just take it slow. I'll give you a call." I patted his shoulder and closed the car door, then headed inside.

However, the next evening, Donald arrived with a bouquet of roses. So many roses that I couldn't even see his face as I watched him from my bedroom window. He tripped a few times, but when I peeked around the hallway corner, he was on one knee in front of Mum. Immediately, the horror set in of what he was about to do.

"Mrs. Cora, you know I love your daughter, and I promise to give her the world from this day forward. Would you grant me permission to offer a proposal of marriage?" His sweat ran down the sides of his face as I watched in dread.

She immediately looked around and caught me hiding. I made hand gestures telling her not to accept, but Cora ignored my displeasure and got caught up in the moment.

"Of course, you have my blessing!" She lifted him off his knees.

Frustrated, I gathered the composure to step out. He stood in the center of the room, dewy from the humidity and nervously awaiting my presence like I was the Queen of England.

"Hello, Jane." He wiped his face with his handkerchief. "I know we've only known each for a short time, but you've changed my world. This evening, I've asked your mother for your hand in marriage. I hope you will accept my proposal. Will you be my wife?"

I felt like a young bride being bought off and sold before my mother.

With little time to think for myself, I sold my soul. "Sure, I'll marry you."

Donald's weak kiss left me lifeless and regretting my decision.

"You'll be so happy!" He grinned, squeezing all my insides.

"Yes, I'm sure." I rested my head over his shoulder and stared into Cora's eyes.

I married Donald out of obligation, not out of happiness.

• • •

Church bells rang one month later at a small chapel near home.

I was a bride in white but black on the inside. After taking our final vow, the liar in me was ashamed, but to appease Cora, I played the role of the doting bride better than Grace Kelly.

The reception had only a handful of people. Most were strangers who barely remembered my name.

• • •

That evening, during our honeymoon, I sulked when we locked lips.

"What's the matter, Jane? You're so tense." Donald rubbed my shoulders as I tried to fantasize past his physique.

"I'm not feeling well," I said, lying back onto the mattress. His eyes salivated on my lingerie.

"Jane, you can't keep refusing me!" He smothered my body and slipped his hand up my negligee.

"Stop it! I can't. I've told you not now, Don!"

I shoved him off and stormed toward the bathroom.

"Come on, Jane! What the hell's wrong with you? We never kiss, we never touch, and all you do is tell me it's never the right time!" He started pounding on the doorframe. "Come out of there, or I'll break the damn door down!"

I crouched in the corner of the bathtub. Fire embers ignited once I shut my eyes. The whorehouse from my childhood appeared. I felt like a prostitute trapped inside a birdcage. From the other side of the door, Donald continued to scream into the crack while he jerked the doorknob.

Finally, an hour later, there was quiet. I unlocked the latch and tiptoed toward the bed, trying not to wake him. I lifted the bed sheets, climbed inside, and remained frozen in guilt.

Our ongoing arguments left me exhausted. Every chance I could, I envisioned John lying beside me. The mirage was pleasant, but it was a cruel indicator of how far off the grid my reality was.

Two months later, I ruptured Donald's ego by moving into the spare room. Intimacy was out of the question. That's when I knew it had to end for good. So, I packed my belongings and left him a note.

I'm sorry I made the mistake of marrying you. —Jane

It was a simple explanation because I knew Donald would have tried anything to reconcile and dissect every word. It was up to Jesus now to give me the strength to face Cora. Heading for Spring Street, I rushed up the steps and forgot what time it was.

"Mum!" I pounded on the porch door. "I know you're in there!" I kept it up until the light turned on.

"What the hell is the matter with you, Jane? We're sleeping—it's midnight." Cora's skin looked like a gray ghost in the moonlight.

"I can't pretend anymore! I don't love him, Mum!" My voice broke.

"Well, don't stand outside like a lunatic! The neighbors already think we're assholes!" she said, covering me up. "Get a hold of yourself."

She pulled up a chair to sit me down. "Talk between sips," she gestured as I pounded back a beer.

There we were at that old, familiar dining table. My childhood tar mat, where I learned about the birds and the bees—and squashed water bugs crawling up my legs in the hot summers.

"So, any thoughts on what you'll do when he comes looking for you?" She raised her eyebrows, then finished the last beer.

"I don't know. I haven't really thought about it. Maybe just do what I did with you and tell him the truth?" I looked complacent, knowing by now he'd already read my letter.

"Well, I have a better idea." She pitched the can into the trash. "Don't say a damn thing. Men have to learn one way or the other. You're ornery, Jane. Just give him a polite smile and knock him out between the eyes. That'll do it." She laughed to her own amusement.

"You know, we think alike."

• • •

After the best sleep I'd had in months, I awoke to Mum hovering over me.

"Well, I was wrong. I tried telling the jackass to stop calling, but he won't stop! Will you do me a favor and invite him over so I can knock him out if you don't have the guts to?"

"OK. Be right there." I squirmed to get loose from the covers and headed for the phone.

"Hello." I yawned.

"Hello? Hello? Is that all you have to say to me?" Don's voice peaked. "You can't stay at your mother's forever. Get your things and come home this instant."

"I'm not coming home, Donald! Don't you get it? I'm not in love with you."

"Don't give me that crap, Jane! You married me, remember? Whether you felt anything or not. And if you think you're just going to pawn me off like some sucker, you've got something else coming!" He sounded as if an earthquake were erupting in his lungs. "Do you hear me?"

"I'm here, aren't I?" I pulled the phone away from my ear to watch Cora making gestures of knocking him out—using a frying pan for his face.

"Donald, we're through. If you need to call your lawyer, send me the bill."

When I hung up the phone, Mum looked proud. She saluted me and flipped over the last pancake. "That's my girl."

But just as I was celebrating my renewed freedom, the phone rang again.

"Hello!"

"Well, hello yourself. Is that how you greet everyone who calls?" John's voice sounded melancholy. "Well, I guess I deserve that."

"Oh, John! Why haven't I heard from you? I've missed you like crazy!" My heart skipped a beat while I slipped around the corner to hide.

"I can't stop thinking of you, Jane."

Although I yearned to be with him. I paused to collect my thoughts. "But I didn't hear from you. I thought we were over?"

"I made you a promise, didn't I? Will you forgive me?"

His tender sincerity made the butterflies in my stomach start up again.

"I have to keep it down; Mum's close."

"I'm in Cleveland. Come see me."

I grabbed a pen from the counter to take down his address.

"I'll pick you up this evening when you get in!"

That night, I quickly packed some things and caught a bus out of Pittsburgh without saying a word.

• • •

As I departed the station, the horizon melted into the clouds like cotton candy—a sweet reminder that John and I would be reunited.

When I arrived, we kissed with both passion and desperation for each other. It was like an old-fashioned movie scene. Feeling his lips again erased the past and led me into a pilgrimage of womanhood I'd never known. I made love vulnerably, exploring the depth of our power together. He was the air I had to breathe.

But back home there was still some unfinished business …

Dear Mum,

I'm sorry I left suddenly, but I know you'll understand why I did.

I'm following my heart and moved to Cleveland to be with John.

Here is the address just in case you want to visit us sometime.

I will write you more details soon.

Please don't be mad. —Jane

John and I were so happy. We could have been the hallmark of true love. Really. I couldn't imagine my life without him. It's as if our souls were intertwined, sealed in fate.

• • •

Later that same day, as I fixed supper, John returned from work eager to hold me in his arms. He picked me up like a delicate doll. I interlocked my hands around his neck like a young bride enchanted by her groom. When he threw me over his shoulders, I cried out in laughter.

He was a blue-collar worker, and I was a girl from the slums. But in that moment, we were richer than life. He ran his fingers down my back and showed a vulnerability that made me feel safe.

"I love you," he said, looking deeply into my eyes.

But before I could say it back, the first gunshots were fired, shattering the glass. John threw me to the floor.

"I know you're in there, you bitch!" Don packed the next round in a hurry.

"Who's that?" John looked over the window ledge, trying to see the intruder.

"If the whore doesn't come out, I'm coming in! And I'll blow both of your goddamn heads off!"

We were trapped with nowhere to run. The only way to escape death was to end my love story and surrender. The rifle's barrel met my forehead as I opened the screen. Donald's obsession had me for ransom as he forced me to my knees.

"Donald don't do this! You and I are over!"

My body trembled as I looked the barrel in the eye and felt the sting from broken glass under my knees.

"Did you forget you were married?" he yelled into my ears, circling me like a ringmaster.

"I'm not in love with you. I'm in love with John."

"You dumb woman, why didn't you hide it from me? Instead of leaving a letter for your mother with your new address?"

He was right. I had handled everything all wrong—and that decision cost me my happiness.

John came closer, his face expressionless. "Explain this to me, Jane."

Donald gripped the trigger, ready to shoot.

"Yes, Jane, why don't you explain to him how you married me and went on to sleep with him?"

Donald immediately pointed the rifle at John's chest.

"Stop it! I'm begging you, Donald. Please don't do this!"

The two men deadlocked in silence.

Crippled with fear, I almost fainted as I watched Donald push the barrel into his chest.

"Get your disgusting face out of here before I put a bullet in his heart."

Stumbling to my feet, I made it to the doorway and prayed he wouldn't murder us.

After I heard Donald's car pull out the driveway, I could see John's countenance die.

"I think you'd better go," he said, removing his emotions.

"Leave? No, John! Please, let me explain!" I dove into a panic. "Look at me! Why won't you look at me?" I screamed gripping his shirt.

"It's over, Jane! Not when you're married." His icy tone stopped short as he grabbed his car keys. "Get the rest of your things and leave."

All I can remember is despair. A terrible pain, like I was drowning inside.

"Don't do this, John!" I jerked the car door, trying to get inside. I lost grip of the handle and fell onto the dirt. Stranded on the side of the road, the smoke covered me in rage thicker than hate as his car disappeared in the distance.

I fell for a lover, deceived my mother by following my heart, and hexed Donald into loving me.

After John left that evening, I waited for hours, hoping for his return. But when there was no sign of him, it was time to pack my belongings and say goodbye.

Taking one last look around the apartment was unbearable. Our dinner was still on the table, and the bed sheets were tangled from the night before. The only thing more painful was that I broke his heart. Goodbye, John.

I never shared a love like that again. Although I deeply cherished my third marriage, I never again felt that passion that I had with John. It was as if the light inside me had burned out the moment he and I were separated. Love is fragile.

• • •

I returned home a divorced black widow. The townspeople knew it. They could sniff it out, but I ignored the noise. Eventually, Donald remarried. And as troubling as it was to acknowledge his insanity when it came to rejection, it provided a sigh of relief that I had survived his obsession.

• • •

Looking forward to a fresh start, I placed a deposit on an apartment downtown, where I paid only fifteen dollars a month. Even then, I was scraping by, trying to survive, nickel-and-diming my way to freedom.

The asphalt jungle was a wild circus of lights. And while the economic boom pitched a snowball of opportunities, the limelight was still dim for women in the world. But I never gave up—not for one second. In fact, I did the opposite. I shoved my way to the top past business suits tendering their eyes on my breasts, and I spoke with tenacity. I had every male boss wrapped around my fingertips.

My inner voice commanded attention, and on quiet days, when the hustle had passed and McKeesport was thriving behind the rotten trenches, my favorite place still was the old cemetery. Built on a hilly mound of moss, the seasons spun like fireflies up there and calmed my worries about tomorrow. I could escape behind the vast estates of tombstones, daydream into sunsets, and comb my fingers on the earth. It's where I allowed my emotions to trickle down the muddy grooves when I needed bravery to heal. John was my past, a place in my heart for me to nurture when the wild calamities brewed a time for mourning.

Colorful kaleidoscopes brightened the sky, leaving my fearless heart to wonder. Although the world around me felt transient, I sensed God surrounding me, pouring his light on my skin and speaking to me in the whispers of the wind. Time can mend the brokenhearted if you allow the healing to start.

That day on the hillside, I did just that. I bid farewell to John, sending a swarm of dandelion petals into the windy currents below and onward to the universe.

Chapter 10

TRASH IN A SILK SUIT

*"When I see men in silk suits, I see an animal farm of idiots.
To me, the majority are predators handing out peanuts. Perhaps it's
my upbringing to blame, or perhaps it's in the drinking water."*

—JANE CORSARO

Months later, I came out from behind the walls of my broken palace. The popcorn ceiling would fall into my soup bowl as I'd overhear my neighbor's weekly marital affairs echoing through the air vents.

It was more entertaining than watching television. And besides, when you have thin walls, it's easy to eavesdrop. My apartment building had become a therapist's nightmare.

Being alone in the world was unnatural for me, but I became great at distracting myself. Already in my mid-twenties, my mind held a wealth of experience. However, the battles were far from over.

My closest friends had gotten married—and just when I assumed things couldn't get worse, they did! Thelma married my brother, Chuck.

She catered to him hand and foot, and Chuck soaked up her kindness like bleach on a candy cane. The more she gave, the more he demanded. But I knew his temper would get the best of him someday, landing Thelma a black eye along with bruises. But she continued to defend him. And when I tried to intervene, she'd deny any wrongdoing and pretend it was an accident.

My heart knew she'd pay the ultimate price. After all, the only way out of a war zone is to admit there is one because, if not, you'll spend your whole life in battle.

I'd had empathy for Thelma. She was naïve and good-hearted—a petite thing with small, twinkling eyes and a radiant smile. People admired her tenderness, but after years of stress, it eventually faded. Thelma loved my brother with every fiber of her being—until his last beating left her nearly unrecognizable. That's when she gave up and divorced him. She remained unmarried from then until the day she died.

• • •

Every relationship left a mark on my spirit and chipped away at my trust—especially those with men—so I fed my soul with other pleasures. A can of beer to calm my anxieties proved a great start. After a long day, the local pub was an easy escape. The jukebox provided me contentment while I sipped slowly, taming the avalanches in my mind. The pub never had a dull moment, and even though ladies weren't encouraged to sit at the bar tops, I went against the rules.

That's when a confident stranger in a silk suit grabbed a seat to join me.

"Well, hel-lo, gorgeous!" He caressed my arm gently. "Hey, bartender, order us a round, will ya?"

I looked over without batting an eye.

"Where's your wife?"

"My wife?" He fiddled with his tie, brushing up against my leg. "She's home where she belongs."

"Don't you think you belong in the doghouse?" I said under my breath, as I took a swig and grabbed my coat.

"Hey now! I respect my wife!" He looked around embarrassed by the attention.

But his arrogance was no match for what was coming to him.

"You respect your wife—but you don't respect me, you son of a bitch!" I slammed down the glass and slapped him across the face.

"What's got into you, whore?" he arose violently.

"Oh, nothing. I just can't stand the smell of pigs!" I cursed, then pushed him backward. Before I knew it, I was being lifted by my underarms and dragged outside.

"Try acting like a lady." The bartender dusted off his pants and tossed over my purse.

"Well, try telling your boys to act like grown men, and maybe ladies won't have to put them in their place!"

That evening, I headed down the lengthy halls of Stone Alley into the dark corridors and toward the cemetery to avoid the muggy heat inside my apartment. In the grassy coolness, I found a soft patch to make a bed. Angered by the altercation, I curled up into a tiny ball. There were women who'd have given him what he wanted. I just wasn't one of them.

And if it hadn't been for work obligations the next morning, I think I'd have stayed and been buried under a tombstone that read:

I FINALLY FOUND PEACE.
LIFE IS TOO COMPLEX.

The new job at G.C. Murphy was average. I sold cosmetics by the truckload to mature women looking for a facelift, a safe disguise to play make-believe with themselves. Who are we anyway when we hide behind our masks? Isn't it better to show our true selves?

I was tired of men being able to do and say as they pleased. Every man in my life felt like the ruler of my domain, and I was nauseous just thinking about it. They didn't try to hide anything. We women had to hide it all.

Chapter 11

THE BEASTS OF THE RIVER

"I was a walking magnet. Everywhere I went, I collected crap!
The solution was drinking a good can of Bud Light."

—JANE CORSARO

As the seasons changed, I would follow miles of trailheads on soul searches, but I wasn't sure what I was looking for.

The riverbeds were surrounded by mystic evergreens, and the twigs that crunched under my toes symbolized breaking bread with God and asking for forgiveness.

When I left G.C. Murphy, I started a new job as a grocery clerk. When there was time to sneak in a daydream or two, I'd envision running away to become an actress. I imagined being covered head to toe in glamourous gowns and drinking wine that trailed down my throat like silk, leaving a satin finish.

Hollywood was a place of glitzy fairy tales, and the legendary starlets of our time went to their graves bejeweled in mystery. But there, in my daydreams, I flowed into the arches of time and remembered my encounter with the traveling woman who had sensed my destiny long ago. Perhaps the actress was harboring inside me and had already mastered the "beasts of the world"? After all, each situation brought out a distinct character within me.

It was the tug of war of power. Hollywood had reminded me of why the Youghiogheny and the Monongahela River collided. Their currents dueled to maintain relevance over each other, just like every star had to fight to make a name. I compared this to the nature of the beast I internalized as I sought independence. Was I at war with myself? At night, when I'd take long walks, these were the thoughts that echoed in my mind. Whether it was pitching rocks or running my fingers along the bark of tree trunks, the exploration brightened my disposition.

• • •

Although the umbrella of Mother Earth was comforting, you can never be too careful when wandering alone in the woods.

With each step, the wooden bridge creaked underneath my feet— and on this night, it could have cost me my life.

It was after dusk. On my way home from work, the fog had covered the lanterns on our pedestrian bridge, making it difficult for me to see. The drifting mist felt as if I were walking into an unknown dimension. Its ghostly cloak sent chills up my spine. Soon after, I heard faint footsteps pressing down on the baseboards. I turned around, alarmed by a tall shadow lurking at the entrance. The figure was carrying a sharp blade in its right hand. Its body movements were foreign, like nothing I'd ever seen before. Horrified, I sprinted as fast as I could, my heart pounding out of my chest. Instinctively, I thought of Mother and imagined that if bloodhounds found my body in the river the next morning, she would have thought I committed suicide.

Gasping for air, my left shoe caught on a nail, ripping it from its sole. I tugged at it to free myself, but after little success, I removed both shoes and ran barefoot up the sharp incline toward the streetlights and neighborhood shops, which were only a few yards away. I was sure that whatever it was would catch me. But when I turned around, the unidentified figure was nowhere to be found. It had vanished.

To this day, I have no certainty if what I witnessed on that bridge was a figment of my imagination or a serial killer lurking around the dark water's edge. For many nights after, I lay awake with anxiety, believing that whatever it was had followed me home. Yet, nothing ever came to surface, not a trace.

"You're lucky it didn't kill you!" my coworker scolded me while lugging a heavy roast above her head. "If I'd seen that freak, I would've jumped off the bridge!" She threw the meat onto the chopping board.

"Janice, trust me, you would've run. Jumping off the bridge is far scarier."

"Well, it's better than being sliced up into tiny pieces! Get real, Jane. Times are changing in this world. People lose their marbles all the time. One minute, things appear normal—and the next, whatever it was wants to cook you for dinner!"

I raised my eyebrows at her crude analogy just as I turned on the slicer.

"You've made your point. Next time, I'll be more careful."

"Say, let's go out this evening. I know a great place just up the street, and there are no creeps lurking around there." She smiled while undoing her apron.

"I don't know. I'm not really into wild parties anymore."

"Jane, look at me. Do I look like a party animal to you? I'm ten years your senior, and I've never missed a day of work in my life. It's wearing on my figure. Haven't you noticed? We'll just go for a quick beer—it'll cheer you up!" she said, grinning as she headed out the door.

That evening, Janice's eyes teared up with laughter at every dirty joke.

"Here's to another year of more meat and long hours!" We laughed.

"Excuse me, ladies, but can I join the party?" A good-looking man smiled. We were charmed and invited him for a round of drinks. Maybe it was his English accent that had me smitten.

"May I have the honor of driving you home this evening?" He placed his hand out as an offering.

"Sounds good. Hey, Janice! If you'll excuse us, I have to open shop early tomorrow," I said, slipping her a cheeky grin.

"Alright, you two! Just get to it!" She winked, throwing her coat over her shoulder and placing a half-smoked cigarette in her mouth. "See you tomorrow!"

I liked the idea of getting to know him, but he was moving a bit faster than I had realized. Immediately, after leaving the parking lot, I could tell there was more on his mind.

"How about we go to my place for a little while?" He rubbed his hand on my upper thigh.

"Not tonight ... I have to be up early tomorrow for work."

"Oh, come on! Don't act so innocent, and besides, we can get to know each other a little better." He resumed moving his hands further up the side of my skirt, calculating his next move.

"I've already told you no! Just pull over and drop me off here!" My patience deteriorated.

"You're a prude!" His eyes caught fire as he stepped on the gas, gaining speed.

"Stop driving so fast—you're going to kill us!" I clawed at the dash, trying to hold on. He turned blind corners, driving us toward the mouth of the river like I was an offering.

While he sped at full throttle, I forced up the lock and kicked open the car door. But I lost my grip, tumbled down the rocky ridge, and plummeted to the side of a ravine, hitting my head on a large boulder. Seconds later, I fell unconscious.

As the sun rose, my eyelids felt like glass shards. I searched for direction. I could hear the raven's call and feel the skylight dilate my pupils as I struggled to keep awake. As I slowly rubbed my head, it seemed as if the earth were spinning in circles. I caught my balance and noticed flashing lights ahead. People were rushing toward me, but I couldn't remember what had happened. All I knew was that I was alive.

The blood on my fingertips trickled down my forehead like aged wine. I felt like the beast of the river had finally devoured me.

Injured from head to toe, I collapsed onto their shoulders as they carried me up the hill and lifted me onto a stretcher, where I refused medical care because they'd nickel and dime me for everything I had. So, they bandaged me up and sent me on my way. The walk home felt like a two-dimensional simulation, neither here nor there, as my head throbbed with malaise.

The nasty concussion took weeks to heal, and all I could remember was falling into the ravine, like Alice down the rabbit's hole. The descent was painful, but the impact saved me from drowning. The Mad Hatter world I was living in was the spellbinding reality that introduced me to many villains and looney characters. One in particular comes to mind.

• • •

You might expect that all my memories would have turned into Jell-O. But I never forgot T-Boo. He was a foreign exchange student from India. Poor fellow, it was his first time in the States. He was still learning English. T-Boo had an abnormal stature, big bushy hair, and bulbous brown eyes that demanded attention. He was driven by adventure and naïve as an opossum.

We were introduced at a community social. He was a year into med school and was raised with a silver spoon in his mouth. Everything we talked about revolved around his luxury estate in India. In fact, he'd pester me every chance he could about where I lived. In his mind, we all had estates.

So, after refusing to escort T-Boo to my father's home for the hundredth time, I finally caved in. It was time he had a lesson in real life. We hopped in his shiny red convertible to head to the land of wholesome living.

I told him my father was famous and that everyone called him Mr. Fish. Little did I know this "lesson" would change T-Boo's life forever.

"Oh, I can't wait to see it!" His eyes were jubilant.

"My home?" I chuckled, assuming that he was joking.

"Not too much farther, T-Boo. Hold your horses."

"Oh, I am so excited to meet the Fish man! Do I have to kiss his hands?" His excitement cut through his accent like a babe in Wonderland.

"No, T-Boo, you just shake hands. But I have to warn you, my estate is much smaller than yours."

"Oh! Well, I'll be the judge of that. I'm sure your castle is quite nice." He rallied forward like a rattlesnake.

Driving up the hillside, the wind blew through my hair as T-Boo's vocal cords belted out his native songs. He was unaware of the adventure awaiting him, but we merrily drove along like a sultan with his Hollywood showgirl.

"You can pull over here." I pointed to the side of the road.

"We're here?" His eyes bulged as he scanned the area.

"Yes, go on and pull over right here." I motioned to the curb and hopped out.

"Oh, my God, this must be a hidden fortress!" He squinted and rubbed his eyes in delight.

"No, T-Boo. It's more like suburbia. Come on, follow me!" I ushered him through the backyard where his innocence got the best of him.

Soon, things took a turn for the worse. Just as we arrived past the hedges, I spotted my father flat on his face, sobering up on a lawn chair.

"Oh! My God, that man's dead!" T-Boo's hair stood up with electricity. "Mr. Fish man is dead!"

He lifted my father's arm, which fell to the ground like dead weight.

"No, silly, he's just taking a nap. He's a deep sleeper—he's had a few beers." I casually nudged him as I walked past Father's lifeless body sprawled on the lawn chair.

"A few beers? My God, he's a dead fish; can't you see he's not moving?" T-Boo looked horrified as I pulled him by the collar to the side of the house to calm him down.

"Fish man is alive T-Boo. He's not a dead fish!" I tried to soothe him with my best Indian accent while handing him a handkerchief from my purse.

Suddenly, T-Boo became frantic. The incident had excited him a little too much.

"T-Boo need to go to bathroom—now!" he groaned, pulling on his trousers.

I looked around. There was no bathroom in sight, and I didn't dare take him inside.

"There's a patch of grass, right over there." I motioned to a mound of thick brush and weeds.

"What in the world is this place? I can't go pee there—the wind will blow it down the hill!" He jerked around with his pants, twisting to contain the urge.

"Just go pee, T-Boo. I won't look," I insisted, trying not to laugh at his frenetic behavior. "Just pee! Pee, T-Boo! Imagine you're at home in your estate." I giggled under my breath as my father lay lifeless, only feet away from the traveling visitor. The two of them were worlds apart but oddly similar. Both carried the stubbornness of tigers and were saturated with pride.

"You live in this place?" He zipped his pants up quickly, looking around like a wild burro and then turning in astonishment.

That's when I finally let him know the truth.

"No, T-Boo! I live in the slums, far away from here—down there, in fact, and my ceiling is caving in!"

I'll admit that my sarcastic nature got the best of me, but it was only to broaden his worldview.

"My God, I have to get out of this place! Not what I thought!" He fussed with his pant legs and bolted for the car as his hair stood up like pine needles.

"Well, it was nice meeting you!" I waved like a pageant queen as he peeled out, tossing my scarf in the dirt.

Just then, my father's wife, Helen, stormed toward me, swinging a hatchet and a chicken's head.

"Why did you bring that man over here?" she screamed with her Russian accent, still swinging the chicken wildly like a piñata.

Thankfully, T-Boo wasn't around for this wholesome introduction. It would have nailed him in his coffin.

"He needed a place to pee, so I thought of you," I said, casually walking down the road, leaving Helen to despise me even more. I turned back for a moment to see her squeeze the chicken's head so tightly from anger that its eyes almost popped out.

Maybe that was payback for when I was a child, or maybe I was proud to showcase my inheritance. Either way, it felt good that I helped clear the air that day.

More crazy escapades occurred throughout my twenties. The only way to describe my young adult life is this: Think fast and never look back.

After dodging a bullet that almost cost me my life and finding comedy in the ignorance of humankind, the only thing left for me to do was dance.

Chapter 12

THE GAPA CLUB

Overnight, I had become the town's reveler, swinging my hips like a disco queen under the limelight.

The Gapa Club was the place to be, while the night roared with lovers and villains from all walks of life. Ruby-red lips kissed the smooth jawlines of city men who lived vicariously through their fantasies. Men circled like sharks, from the grandiose to the mobsters. All simulating a bite, but to no glory. I resisted the temptation.

"My friend wants to dance with you!" A corky, blond-haired man with a curly mustache pinched my arm.

"What man?" I turned around in circles, distracted by the mirror ball above my head.

"My friend, Joe—the guy with the curly black hair over there." He grabbed my hand to guide me over.

We were introduced quickly, and before the song ended, I learned that Joe was a star football player from the local college. After a night of dancing, he invited me back to his apartment.

But it was too good to be true, and the infatuation came to a shrieking halt. Just as we were sinking into the cushions of his love seat, his girlfriend walked in unexpectedly.

"I thought you were away for the weekend?" He acted surprised, buttoning up his shirt. But her quirky disposition vanished when she caught me rising from behind the popcorn bowl.

"Who's this broad? Another tart from down the street?" She bolted at me like an addict on heroin—wielding a spatula as her weapon. "Get out of this house, you tramp!" She swiped at me.

"I didn't know he had a girlfriend!" I threw the popcorn bowl into the air to defend myself.

Joe stormed into the bathroom, leaving us to spar. Almost losing my balance, I dodged each swing, bobbing and ducking down the flight of stairs and into the alleyway where she spit at my backside.

"And don't come back!" she shouted, marking her territory like an alley cat.

"I'm not the one you should be running after—he's the asshole!" I yelled up, taking a moment to catch my breath.

She leaned on the stair banister and slipped the spatula inside her belt, like a western outlaw. "You're the third lady I've caught him with, you know that?" She huffed.

"And I won't be his last! Maybe it's time to kick him to the curb instead of chasing all these women down his stairwells." I wiped my nose and turned to find a cab home, leaving her some food for thought.

I never looked back, but moments later, I could hear them arguing from their upstairs window.

The men of the Gapa era were like onions. Their allegiance to woo me seemed enticing at first, but the more I peeled back their layers, the more they stunk and made my eyes burn.

Anthony, the rugged gangster from New York who was in town on business, was one of those men. We had bumped into each other on the way to the restroom at the club. His accent impressed me, but his tongue didn't, especially when he bragged about all the men his mob pinched and threw in the back of his trunk. We only went out three times before he shot himself in the foot. What a winner.

His cousin Eddie called to let me know the gory details.

"I'm sorry, but Anthony can't pick you up tonight. He shot himself in the foot."

"What kind of gangster is he?" I said, undoing my rollers. "Tell him to ice it and leave the big guns to real men. We're over!" I slammed down the phone, never to hear from Anthony or, thankfully, the mob again.

More than ever, I was becoming like my mother, spitting out men like sunflower seeds and avoiding the nuts.

• • •

I needed a break from the Gapa Club, so I tried a new place on the other side of the river. Janice and I were both dressed to kill, but as we approached the dance hall, we saw it was closed.

"Hello, ladies. Where you headed?" The voice grabbed our attention.

We both turned to see a young man only a short distance away, gazing at us mysteriously and leaning on a damaged fence. He had prominent features, both handsome and unusual, a gaunt face with hazel eyes, pillowy lips, and an impoverished frame.

"I work at Mayview, just up the road. It's my day off, so I'm just trying to find something to do around here," he said, catching up to us.

"Mayview?" I asked, looking intrigued.

"I know what you're thinking. Mayview, the mental hospital. It frightens many people, but it's actually quite nice once you've been there as long as I have. You get used to it."

We continued down the road.

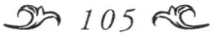

"Well, we were just looking for a place to go dancing, other than the Gapa Club. What's your plans tonight?"

"Oh, me? Well, I'm just taking a stroll. I enjoy people-watching, particularly seeing the way they interact with life. How they breathe, how they struggle. It's beautiful, don't you think? To know our own mortality and existence?" His eyes shone, appearing lost in thought.

"Can we go to Mayview?" Janice tugged my coat like a child.

"Well, sure you can! Just give them my name tomorrow when you arrive, and I'll give you a tour."

His smile was flirtatious but deviant.

"Well, what name should we give them?" I asked, enchanted by his candor.

"Ernie. Ernie Clemmons." He anxiously shook my hand. "It was nice to meet you, ladies! You'll love it up there. The views are incredible, and the people aren't as crazy as you may think." He waved and then vanished before I could set a time.

"Interesting character," I said under my breath.

"Jane, this will be an adventure—we have to go!" Janice persisted.

That night it was hard to sleep with the sounds of cop cars racing down our streets. I tossed and turned under the covers, thinking of Mayview Mental Hospital and the phantoms that filled its hallways.

Later the next day, as we drove up the rugged path, I saw the fortress in the distance. The red brick walls were surrounded by tall hedges. The ash in the air created the perfect storm. I could sense something lurking beneath its deceptive façade ... eternal madness. The day was uncomfortably hot, yet the sky was drained of color as we reached the reception desk to ask for Ernie.

"Oh, hi! We're here for our tour." I looked through the thick plexiglass barrier.

A statuesque man rose from his chair, his skin loosely hanging over the sides of his chin, his mouth turned upside down with an insidious frown.

"Whom are you wishing to see?" His sleepy eyes awoke as his breath fogged the glass.

"Ernie, Ernie Clemmons. He told us to meet him here and said he would give us a tour?" I gulped, swallowing my insides when I saw his deformed features.

"Ha, ha, ha, ha. Foolish girls." He sunk back into his chair to write.

"Well, what's so funny? Hey, c'mon! Why are you ignoring us?" I hit the glass with my palm.

"Ernie doesn't work here—he's a patient!" He pounded his fist on the table, then smeared the ink against the glass with his dirty palms to scare us away.

"But we just spoke to him the other day. That can't be. He said he worked here!" I argued.

"Naïve little girls. Tsk, tsk." He continued to shake his head. "Do you believe everything you hear from strangers?"

"Well, no." I hesitated and looked back at Janice, who appeared nervous and was shivering.

"Ernie's been here for many years. The man hears voices, for God's sake! Don't believe in all the fairytales, ladies. Believe only what your gut tells you." He grabbed a cloth and slowly wiped his fingers, one by one. "These men are no longer men anymore if they're inside here." He placed the cloth aside to move his pencil over the registry book of patients and stopped at Ernie's name so I could see it.

"Their minds have been abducted—taken hostage by the devil." He slammed the book shut. "The cops found him wandering around town last night. These patients always find a clever way to get out. You're lucky he didn't cut you open like lemons," he said, his voice pungent.

My body felt numb with fear as I stepped away from the window in shock.

"Thank you, sir. We'll be leaving now."

And as quickly as we came, we ran out. Janice fell to the ground, laughing from panic. "That man could have killed us!"

I paused to look up at the rocky tower that protected us from Ernie and felt lucky to be alive. "Yes. Somehow, I knew that all along. Now let's get out of here!" I helped her onto her feet.

After almost losing my skin and running from the sharks, I realized that the world was full of them. Deep into the gauntlets of our psyche, we could all become Ernie's and gangsters.

Back at the grocery store, I sliced into red meat, often wondering what had strayed in Ernie. Was it the loneliness, the abuse, or the solitude of his thoughts that provoked him to fade from society? The meat rested as I turned off the blade, leaving me sickened by Ernie's infatuation with death.

I was tired of running, just like Ernie. And I was tired of hiding from my landlord, who'd stalk me for rent whenever I was a few dollars short.

"You're five bucks short this month—you'll either pay, or I'll evict you!" She squinted through the peephole. On the other side, I could see her large protruding teeth and gums chomp away on tobacco. Then I let her have a piece of my mind.

"Say, did you ever eat corn on the cob through a picket fence?" I popped my bubble gum loudly, throwing her off guard.

Hell-bent on ruining my day, she served me the papers.

"That's it! You've got thirty days to vacate!" She opened her pocket mirror to check her teeth.

"Sounds good to me!" I slammed the door.

• • •

The battle to persevere and choose sanity over insanity felt like tackle football inside my mind. It would have been easier to hide in a ditch than face my demons.

I had a home for now, but tomorrow held no promises. I was always moving from one place to the next. My mind could tolerate a lot, along with the ceiling falling into my soup bowls, and even the sirens that kept me awake at night. But if there was one thing I couldn't stand, it was seeing cockroaches swinging from the rafters like trapeze artists. I might have been poor, but I was always clean!

Chapter 13

SUGAR AND SPICE

"Man had placed himself in the lowest of low places, a radical circle of hate, pinning us against each other in order to create boundaries and segregation. I didn't understand the divide between our flesh. We all bleed the same color and will all die someday."

—JANE CORSARO

After the grocery store went out of business, Janice and I grew apart. She worked on the other side of town, and I was at the factory, working some of the longest and most intensive hours of my life.

My body ached after hours of packaging merchandise while earning quarters by the hour. I felt like an old maid, picking at my skin that had developed clusters of red bumps from stress. Depressed by my appearance, I rarely went outside. Instead, I took shelter on the third floor of a rundown apartment complex with shared lavatories.

For three years, I was a recluse, surviving on canned meals and bathing while standing up to limit other residents' dirty soap scum from seeping into my skin. I felt naked inside and spiritually dark. The women in the factory were all spinsters, rough around the edges, heavyset gossipers, with their noses in the air. Their jealousy must have fed their egos as they engaged in making constant remarks about my skin.

That was until I finally shut them up for good.

"Jane, what did you do to your face? It looks like someone exfoliated you with cherry sauce!" They quacked away like geese.

"I know, her face looks like the Red Sea, only it's boiling over!" another said, and they fell over in laughter.

Calmly, I placed my apron on the line and undid my hair tie, shaking it loose, so they could see my beautiful waves unfold. And with poise and the utmost dignity, I gave them a little piece of me.

"Did you know your nose touches your upper lip?" I said to one woman who looked mortified as she touched her mouth. "And you! You're so short, it's a wonder the city doesn't fine you since your ass touches the street, leaving a trail of filth!"

My eyebrows raised as I siphoned their insides. The two women were at a loss for words as I bid them farewell. "Do me a favor, will ya? Let our boss know I quit."

Once it was all over, I found that cleaning homes became an enjoyable escape, earning just enough money to purchase my first vehicle and cover the rent. My acne cleared a few months later, and I was happier than I'd been in a long time.

Taking long drives and letting the wind blow through my hair was exhilarating. It was like winning an Oscar because I kept discovering another side of me.

• • •

As I made my way through town one day, I bumped into my older cousin, Virginia. She was a plain woman with barely a personality. She was religious, soft-spoken, and simply dressed.

"How have you been, Jane?" Her meek voice struggled to carry her frame.

"Oh, I've been good. Couple bumps in the road but still alive." I laughed obnoxiously as we strolled along.

"Well, that's good to hear. Would you like to come by this afternoon? We have a family friend coming over later. I would love for you to meet him. It's been such a long time, Jane," she said, sweetly looking like a young Mother Teresa.

"That would be nice."

So that day I went home to freshen up, put on my favorite shade of red lipstick, and since it was warm outside, dressed in shorts and a floral crop top.

"Hi, Virginia!" I smiled through the screen door, barely able to see her silhouette.

"Hello, Jane." She quickly ushered me inside, as if to hide me from the neighbors. "Jane, what on earth are you wearing?"

"What am I wearing?" I laughed. "I'm wearing an outfit appropriate for summer."

Virginia placed her finger over her lips to quiet me down.

"Our pastor is coming over! Put on my long dress and blouse." She sequestered me to the back room for observation.

Instantly, my temper exploded before Jesus.

"So, you're telling me the pastor isn't here to preach but take me to bed?" I raised my voice, startling her expression. "What's wrong with these pastors nowadays? A woman can't wear an outfit without being sexualized?" My insides were rising like a mushroom cloud.

"Jane! Your language!" She struggled to pray over me as she walked me toward the door, just as the pastor was pulling up the driveway.

"Perfect timing, isn't it?" I looked back at Virginia with displeasure.

"Hello, ladies." He reached out to shake my hand.

"She's staying; I'm leaving! I guess some of us are more appropriate to be around male testosterone levels. The Lord already knows you want to take me to bed!" I shouted while looking over at her neighbors eavesdropping.

The pastor looked astonished.

"Have a nice day!" I said, blowing him a kiss and hitting the gas pedal.

Driving out of town, I tried to calm the fire that fueled my frustration. I wanted to meet people without religious expectations or preconceived agendas. So, I went to the only place where I knew everyone was welcome. On the outskirts of town was a tiny dive bar. No one knew me there, so it was like starting from scratch.

The pub had a raw stench, but the ambience was quite pleasant. It was full of city folk looking for a haven and a place to stay undetected.

I looked across the room, trying to find a seat, but it was packed wall to wall.

"You can sit here!" A young lady waved at me.

"Are you sure?" I pointed at myself, shooing away the smoke.

"Sure, but my girlfriend will be back in a minute. Pull up a seat and join us." Her tongue licked up the salt around her margarita glass.

"Thanks!"

"You're so beautiful," she said, admiring my dress.

"Thank you. You're the first person in a long while to say that." I looked away, blushing from her forthcomingness. "I'll be right back—I'm heading for the ladies' room!" I gestured.

"OK!" She nodded and took another sip of her drink.

Little did I know I was being watched.

As I entered the restroom, there were only two small stalls available. I crammed inside and hovered over the toilet seat. And since the room was so dark and narrow, I had to be careful not to snag my stockings. As soon as I flushed, there was a loud bang on my door.

"Hey! You in there! Come out!"

Quickly pulling up my undergarments, I unlocked the stall door, disgruntled by the ruckus. I immediately had to dodge a woman's fist coming for my head.

"What's the matter with you?" I swung my purse wildly to block her masculine frame.

"I caught you flirting with my girl!" She pinned me in between two sinks.

"You're gay?" My mouth dropped like a caught fish. "Look, I just wanted a place to sit, and she offered me a seat." I rambled along to calm her jealousy and save my throat.

"You're not gay?" Her pupils began to dilate, and her hands released from my dress collar.

"No, I'm not. Now, will you please excuse me? I've got better things to do than be held up in some bathroom."

After exiting, I made eye contact with her girlfriend, who had innocently let me join her company. But instead of walking over to explain what had transpired, I simply nodded and left my drink behind as a peace offering to the misunderstanding.

I learned this: When you search for belonging, choose whom you surround yourself with wisely. If you don't, you may end up in the wrong seat.

• • •

After my shenanigans almost garnered me a black eye, I got word a former coworker of mine, was moving back from Albany, New York. She told me to meet her at the Greyhound station where she had some news to share. She was involved in a nasty divorce and told me she bought a one-way ticket for herself and her children.

As I waited for her, I sat there entertained by all the passengers hopping on and off to new destinations. The Greyhound was the central gateway for businesses and leisure, a low-cost transit to get you to your next refuge or utopia.

While awaiting her arrival, a Black family—a man with his children—were quick to engage me. He looked overcome by emotion, ecstatically lauding me for my bravery. But why?

"You're sitting on the wrong side." The man's baritone voice amplified across the aisle as he pointed upward.

The noise from the train station only added to my confusion as I stood up to read the sign swaying above my head.

"You're in a segregated station, ma'am. You belong on the other side. Blacks sit here." His voice quieted—probably from all the years of conditioning.

I looked back at him and his children. They undoubtedly were wondering about my next move.

Giving in to a system that told us what to do, whom to love, and whom to hate was never an acceptable answer. So, I did what was right. I went into the Black restroom and returned to the same seat. In my mind, I imagined what the newspapers would say—that I was killed by an angry white mob. But it would have been worth the sacrifice to defend freedom.

I'll never forget the man's face. There was hope resurrected by my action, and immediately, one of his children rushed over to place her tiny hand on mine.

"Look how beautiful we are together," she said innocently, then rushed back to swaddle her father's leg.

She was right. We're so much more beautiful together.

As I waited, it made me realize the discrimination I felt from others in my life. My rose-colored lenses were removed to the racist propaganda I didn't always witness, since most of my friends were white. As the family boarded the bus that evening, their father looked back at me, nodded his head in gratitude, and smiled. We were two people looking for salvation in a crowded room. Society wanted to separate us, but I chose to break borders.

I found out my co-worker's Greyhound had arrived, but she wasn't on it. Come to find out, she had stayed back, fearing her husband would take custody of the children. She was like so many women who were afraid to leave their husbands back then. My heart was heavy for her. The shape-shifting journey we were all on left us with scars even though we were heroes for pushing through. We dreamed of making something of ourselves, a hopeful intent blistered by the control of our husbands.

She was trapped in her marriage and not seeing her come off the bus that evening made me realize her problems were far too complex for her to escape. But the scenario didn't leave me without wisdom. A moment in history that defined our fight for equality in a world that segregated us by color, sex, and creed. Women were always displayed as sugar and spice, but the hidden black widow within us was lethal. And one day, I knew we would rise above the oppression and have our voices heard.

Chapter 14

SLOPPY SECONDS

After years of living in McKeesport, I decided it was time to spread my wings. It wasn't until I paid my last month's rent and mustered the courage to move to Norfolk, Virginia—a town I heard was bustling with new opportunities—that I was renewed.

Keeping optimistic, I knew that starting a new job as a cocktail waitress fit the ticket. It was exhilarating, releasing the ball and chain of small-town life.

Skirting around between tables to take orders was a cinch, and eventually, it landed me a table of wealthy men and an interested suitor. That's when I met Leo, a studio photographer and reputable chef. He caught my attention at first glance. Leo was six feet tall and admired for his handsome good looks and magnetic sex appeal. His smooth disposition and hearty compliments had me smitten.

"You're gorgeous when you smile." He delicately touched my hand as I set down another round of drinks.

Entranced by his plush compliments, I smiled and carried on while his cohort's discussed politics and smoked cigars. I'd catch him now and again making eye contact.

Leo was confident, a no-nonsense kind of guy with a daring outlook on life, a man who had to have it all or nothing.

Before I could even place down the bill, he asked me out on our first date. After a handful of weekend vacations, he'd convinced me that he was the one—not to mention his divine cooking and incredible photography that also won my heart.

"Let's spend the rest of our lives together." Leo rose like an eagle over my body, kissing my face. "We'll go to North Carolina and elope."

"You haven't even asked me to marry you yet!" I giggled, climbing on top of him.

"Jane Louise Quinn, will you be my wife?"

His abruptness took me by surprise. He was serious.

"Of course, I'll marry you!" I playfully hit him with a pillow and fell onto his smooth chest to daydream about our life together.

That year, Leo gave me the most beautiful wedding. We found the perfect intimate location in the heart of North Carolina. It was just him and me, but it was everything I had always wanted. Had Cora known, she would have given her approval because Leo had a bank account the size of the state.

However, in the back of my mind, I questioned if I'd committed too soon. Something with Leo's cool demeanor appeared almost criminal—but in that moment, I would have appeared ungrateful to question his generosity in providing me a good life.

Before I realized it, I was living in upper society, above the poverty line for the first time, and fantasizing about motherhood. After moving to Washington D.C., Leo's busy schedule left me time to explore the city and indulge in some self-discovery.

An ad in the Washington Post quickly caught my attention. They were hiring a writer. Though I had little experience, I didn't let that hold me back. Instead, I put on my best business attire, stopped procrastinating, and marched in with my resume. The receptionist immediately ushered me to the back office to meet the president of the company, whom I'd overheard was the top in his field. A deep breath prepared me before I shook hands with his ego. His eyes scanned me from head to foot while he took seconds to glance at my resume.

"Come back Monday. You're hired." He looked around for his coffee.

"Thank you! You won't be disappointed!" I promised, straightening up as I saluted him out the door.

This was all too good to be true, I thought, as I looked up at the building's stealthy exterior. I shimmied in excitement and raced home for my next appointment with my fertility doctor.

Dialing his number, I bit my nails with anticipation to hear the results.

"Congratulations, Jane, you're pregnant." His calm demeanor eased my anxiety. Finally, I could breathe a sigh of relief.

"Thank you, Doctor! Leo will be so excited to hear the news."

After hanging up, I rejoiced and rushed to the bathroom mirror. Lifting my shirt to admire my belly, it was remarkable to know I was creating another life. The day outside was perfect for a stroll, so I grabbed my coat to take a walk in the park.

The brisk fall was blowing the leaves around the lawns as I harmonized to my own tune. As soon as I found a quiet place to rest, I soaked in the sounds of laughter coming from the playground. Each child was a miracle, as were the sparrows perched on the sparse branches.

I looked around with fresh perspective, then caught sight of my husband's car in the distance. Waving my arms in wild anticipation, I quickly noticed that it pulled over near a corner shop.

"That's strange." I squinted to adjust my vision.

Leo stepped out of the driver's seat and made his way to the passenger door. He looked over his shoulder apprehensively while escorting a young woman, leading her up the block in a cyclone of deceit. As soon as I saw the tall blonde's frame, a splinter edged its way into my heart. From what I could see, she was elegant and beautiful with an hourglass figure and a face as soft as an angel. They began to kiss like no one was watching. And that no one was me.

Everything muted, even the laughter of children. Unable to look away, I saw a cab pull up to carry off his mistress, and I was left with their secret, an ugly scar that would never heal.

I hurried back to our apartment. Soon afterward, Leo smugly opened the door, looking uninterested in my presence. He coughed slightly and threw down his car keys.

"What's with you? It looks like you've seen a ghost." He shuffled through the mail.

"I have seen a ghost." I frowned, trying to compose my emotions, but instead, I lost it and charged at him hysterically. "How could you?" I beat his chest while taking in the sweet perfume that wasn't mine on his shirt. "You son of a bitch! Who is she?"

Leo looked dissatisfied and unremorseful as he grabbed my tiny wrists to hold me still. I was no use for him anymore. His appetite for younger blood was apparent, and he needed his supply from someone else. Someone who could give him a quick thrill and build up his enormous ego.

"It's none of your goddamn business!" He smacked me across the face.

For a moment I lost sense of reality and crumbled.

"You told me you loved me." My hands maneuvered to protect my stomach.

"That's right. I did tell you I loved you, but some things change," he smirked coldly, undoing his tie and draping it over the chair.

"We're pregnant." My voice trailed off. And I went to wipe the blood from my nose as I tasted the metallic aftermath of his anger.

"Clean yourself up. You look terrible right now." He paused before heading to the back room.

Overcome with rage, I rushed toward the bedroom door, banging on it till my knuckles bled, but he ignored me.

"We're pregnant!" I slapped my palms over and over against the solid frame door, but he left me in silence, and I fell to the floor sobbing.

That following Monday, I turned down the job at the *Washington Post*. It might have been the greatest opportunity in my career, but I was dead inside. The only life I had was living inside me.

• • •

After learning of Leo's many affairs, I would stay just until I made enough money to leave for good. Cora had called a few times to check in, but I only mentioned how content we were and how far along I was in my pregnancy. Mum didn't know it, but she'd become my saving grace in a time of deep depression.

"Are you sure you're OK, Jane? You sound crummy." I could hear her washing the dishes on the other end.

"No, Mum. I'm just exhausted." I sniffled softly.

"Well, I know you, Jane Louise Quinn, and your mother can tell when you're not happy. What did the asshole do now?" She waited silently for a response.

Cora was just too good, too sharp for these things. And since she had gone through her fair share of assholes, she was no fool to my situation.

"I have to go, Mum. I'll call again soon." I went to pull the covers over my tired body, but she stayed on the phone.

"Jane, listen to me. I'm your mother, damn it! I know I've messed up, but I'm here now, aren't I? And I know what kind of daughter a woman like me pushes out. It's a daughter who doesn't put up with any horseshit. Get rid of him. You've got more strength than me, don't you realize that? Nothing is ever worth sacrificing your happiness for. Nothing. Do you hear me?"

I heard her puff on her cigarette.

"Yes, I hear you, Mum."

After our phone call, I climbed out of bed and looked at myself in the reflection across the room. My hair was a mess, and my body felt like it had been to war. Mum was right. She had always been a breath of fresh air, even when I wanted to resist her advice. I took a long, hot shower to wash the waste of my anger down the drain, and I marveled at the tiny miracle that was growing inside me.

That afternoon, I cut off all my emotions for Leo. I got myself dolled up and carried myself above my heart because I knew my child's future depended on it.

• • •

McKeesport, Pennsylvania Hospital

A month later, I received news that my father was dying. I managed to travel back and forth on my allowance, leaving Leo to continue his affairs back home.

"Stop blowing smoke in his face!" I fanned the lingering scent of ash away from my father's bedside. "Let's step outside, Mum." I tugged her arm and pulled her away from his hospital bed.

"I didn't mean to upset you, Jane. I'm addicted to these hell's sticks," she said, rifling through her purse like a child in search of candy.

"Well, here is not the place—put it out! By the way, does he know yet?"

"I don't think Helen has told him anything. The cancer is too far along."

I peered back into the hospital room at the tubes entering my father's veins.

Mum gave a somber sigh and looked for another cig. "The doctors continue trying new drug therapies to cure the cancer, but nothing's working."

Fatigued from all the stress, I needed to clear my thoughts, so I paced up and down the hospital corridors, passing by patients' rooms. They looked relieved to see a visitor's face. I smiled back but continued to question what the stress would do to me and my unborn child if I didn't rest.

I headed past the nurse's station to rest by my father's side. Mum had left for the night, and Helen was preparing his funeral arrangements.

For once, it was just my father and me. My fingers ran over the rough parts of his knuckles. His eyes shifted back and forth as if he were dreaming, but they never opened to make contact.

"I hope you can still hear me, so I'll start with this." I steadied my voice, searching for the perfect gift of comfort before my final goodbye. "It's Jane, Father. I'm your daughter with the same green eyes as you. Right now, all I have left to say is … I love you so much—and it's OK if you can't say it back because I already know you do."

My voice caved in grief as I stood over his frail body. "I forgive you." It was the only thing left to say.

The machine continued to force oxygen into his lungs as I watched him struggle to survive. And just like that, I felt his hand squeeze mine. It removed years of separation in one breathtaking moment of clarity to know my father had heard me. God had entered the room, and the child in me bid him farewell. "I'll be a good little girl," I whispered through the tears. "Goodbye, Daddy."

Father's passing caused an earthquake inside me. Of all the things to get the best of Fish, I would have never imagined it would be this. It could have been the devils of Brick Alley or the heartbreak from Cora … but it was not the jungles of McKeesport that took his life. It was cancer.

Now he'd be laid to rest in this unruly world without the retirement he had worked so hard for. Father was a warrior for lasting this long, unlike so many who would perish the same way.

. . .

The day we laid my father to rest, it was December 1964. It was an unbearably quiet service with only a handful of people to pay their respects. I stood over Father's silk casket and couldn't bring myself to release my hands from around his fingers. That is, until I heard someone cry out in agony, and that someone, I realized, was me.

Tears streamed down my face—as the actress exposed herself to her audience. The suffocating pain from my heartache felt like bullets being forced out of my soul. All I wanted was my father back!

I didn't care that I had endured years of suffering. Even though my father had barely looked me in the eye most of my life, my love for him was unconditional. Nothing else could separate that bond—not heaven or purgatory or anything in-between.

Like a record player scratching at the surface, I repeated his name over and over again as I cried in isolation. The anguish and trauma from that experience tied my lungs in knots until I blacked out. But, somehow, I was transformed beyond the crisis with eternal power to survive without him. I surrendered to God. And from that moment forward, my faith was unbreakable.

On the flight home, I remained quiet in thought, as I gazed out at the clouds. Up here I felt closer to my daddy.

. . .

My plane touched down in D.C. before dawn. I gathered my things and grabbed a taxi back to a place that was no longer my home, but I had to be resilient.

Arriving on the front doorstep, an underworld grew in my gut and left me nauseous with disgust. I entered quietly, not wanting to wake up Leo. But the sounds of lovemaking whipped my heart as I set down my suitcase and removed my coat and hat.

The bedroom door was left slightly ajar, just enough for me to see hell at its finest and to hear the voices of two women engaged in a threesome with my estranged husband. Lucifer's sex ring had overpowered them into an inferno, just like Brick Alley.

After watching them serenade each other in nakedness, I headed for the kitchen to cook breakfast as if nothing had happened.

The two young women crept out of his lair, covering themselves with my bathrobes.

I turned around to face them.

"Good morning. What would the two of you like for breakfast?" I gave them a frozen smile. They seemed mortified by my kindness.

"We were ... um ... just—" One of them stood there, tongue-tied.

"Never mind that. I'm sure you're all famished." I started the coffee and cracked the eggs on a hot skillet. "Coffee?"

"Sure ... coffee sounds good," the other one said, looking equally confused and awkward.

Leo eventually came out, dressed in his finest business suit, and patted them on the rear before they squealed off like pigs, leaving their coffee behind.

I sipped the last of what was left and celebrated my acting abilities, like a Spartan warrior queen, because at least my soul was still intact—unlike his.

Mum was right. Never settle. And never stay for sloppy seconds.

Chapter 15

ALFIE

"Love shared between a parent and their child is immeasurable.
It is the most beautiful journey you'll ever know."

—JANE CORSARO

The summer after my father died, my son was born. It was 1965, and it was a rebirth of sorts for me, making way for forgiveness for things in the past and ushering in the greatest joy I'd ever known.

Craigy cooed whenever I made my silly faces. His big smile showed off his pink gums whenever he'd giggle or kick around joyfully. I cradled him in my arms, captivated by the enormous love I felt for this tiny miracle. He was perfect.

When the divorce papers were signed, I found an average apartment back home where I was closer to Mum. I took care of my son and myself while receiving government aid for the first time. Leo had made a few phone calls after Craig's birth, but he stopped calling after I refused to leave the baby with my mother and go away on one of his fantasy trips. Those days were over, and I was fine with the maturity I had gained.

As Craig grew older, he amazed me with his intelligence. He was assertive and empathetic, like a wise old soul sitting on my right shoulder. He always seemed to know when his mommy was having a rough day.

Craig was gentle and sensitive to every living thing, even the creatures he'd collect from our backyard.

"Look, Mommy! A frog!" His eyes lit up as if he'd discovered gold.

"Oh, sweetie, he's beautiful. What should we name him?" I ran my fingers through his thick hair.

"He told me his name was Alfie!" Craigy jumped up and down, clasping the tiny frog.

"Well, before Alfie is a part of the family, we'll have to give him a bath."

He followed me to the wash sink, climbed on the stool, and gazed at God's creation. Alfie croaked as I washed and patted him dry.

"Can he sleep in my bed tonight?" His hands clung to my nightgown.

"Well, maybe not in your bed, sweetie. Poor Alfie might get lost. Why don't we build him his own house?" I said, trying to find a box. "Look, we'll use this one. Go on and place him in here."

Craigy puffed his lips at the thought. "But he'll need a blanket—or he'll get cold tonight!"

"Don't worry. Mommy will find him a blanket. Let's see, what can we use?" I searched around, trying to find something soft.

"He can use this!" Craigy ran over to me with a small piece of baby wipe.

"I think Alfie needs something a little thicker. Let's use this instead." I placed a small handkerchief over Alfie as he hopped around the box.

"Alright, your turn. It's bedtime," I said, turning down the lights.

Craig snuggled in right beside Alfie.

"Mommy, what do frogs eat?" Craig looked up curiously.

"I suppose they eat tiny insects that live outside with him." I kissed his forehead gently.

"But why not people food? Those poor *insinects*; they want to live too!" Craigy looked displeased while he sucked his thumb.

"People food sounds a lot better, doesn't it? But that's the way of life, Craigy. Living things have to eat other living things to survive."

"That doesn't make sense," he said. "Then why haven't we eaten Grandma?"

"Oh, Craigy, you'll understand one day." I chuckled. "Now, let's get some sleep. Alfie needs his rest like you, so you both can grow up to be big and strong. Nighty night, sweetheart."

"Goodnight, Mommy."

His tiny head pushed into the pillow as the sounds of Alfie's croaking lulled him to sleep.

That morning he was up early, having had a hard night's sleep, tossing and turning from his allergies. He yawned as he scratched his tender nose.

"Here, honey, it's time for your medication." I playfully spun the spoon around, portraying the moon landing, careful not to spill the syrup.

"Zoom!" Craigy laughed. "Look, Mommy, I landed on the moon!" He balanced a Cheerio on his tongue.

"Amazing! What a bright boy you are. Now let's hurry it up. We have to catch the space shuttle." I picked up his lunch bag as I scooted him toward the door.

"But what if Alfie misses me?" He stopped and peeked between my legs toward Alfie's box.

"Alfie will be just fine. He'll keep Mommy company today." I swung him around. "Have a good day at school, my big first-grader.

And remember to learn lots and lots!" I gave him a hug, squeezing his down winter jacket and nudging him toward the door.

Watching his little nose pressed against the glass took me back to 1st Ward when my father's truck peeled down the driveway. I shook the memory from my mind and waved to Craig as the bus faded away into the distance.

"Well, I guess it's just you and me." I looked over for Alfie's ribbit of approval.

· · ·

Later that afternoon, I greeted Craig at the bus stop. He charged me with enthusiasm, clinging to me tightly and kissing the side of my cheek before we headed to the park to roll down the hillsides.

We tumbled down to the flat ground below like Jack and Jill under the sunshine. Craig crawled on top of my belly, squealing in delight.

"Pinned you! I win, I win!"

"Oh, no you don't!" I growled like a monster, then tickled his sides and lifted him up above me.

As he laughed aloud, I saw the clouds cascade over his head, forming a crystal white halo. Craig was my angel.

It was just the two of us for years. And even though we had our limitations, we still got by, taking a bus into town, playing outside for hours, and going to his favorite place, the town's amusement park, to ride the roller coaster.

Our world was full, fuller than it had been in months—until Alfie passed away.

"Mommy!" Craig screamed from his bedroom.

"What is it?" I quickly dropped the dishes, leaving the water running over them.

"Mommy, why won't Alfie play with me?" He looked down at him, shaking the box. I looked at Craigy's mournful eyes with a sigh.

"Come here, Craigy; sit on Mommy's lap." I patted my legs. His tears stopped momentarily as he rested his head against my chest.

"Honey, Alfie has gone home to be with the other creatures in Heaven." I caressed his back, trying to ease the shock.

"But this is his home. Why can't he stay with us?" He started to cry again.

"Because he's on a journey ... beyond the sunset, sweetie."

"Well, what's beyond the sunset?" He wiped his eyes.

"Love with God in Heaven. All things go beyond the sunset. It's past the moon and stars, and way far away from here. It's a place you can't see or touch, but it always lives inside your heart."

"Can astronauts reach there?" He looked up with hope. "I want to be an astronaut and go beyond the sunset!" He pointed to the sky.

"Oh, honey, you'll be a wonderful astronaut someday, but Mommy needs you down here to snuggle with me some more." I pulled him closer as he wrapped his arms around my shoulders, burying his face to wipe away his sniffles.

"OK, Mommy, we can watch the sunsets together and say hi to Alfie. I know he'll hear us—I'm sure of it!" He dried his eyes on my collar.

"Of course, he'll be able to hear us. Alfie knows how much you loved him, sweetheart." My nose tickled his.

"Can he sleep in our garden?" He pointed outside our window.

"I think that would be nice," I said.

"Thank you, Mommy. You know how to fix everything." Craig's soft skin pressed into my face.

That morning, we carried Alfie outside. The dew from the early morning made the earth soft and moist. There, in a small area beside some flowers, we dug a hole and placed our tiny friend inside.

"Won't he be cold? Can we put the blanket on him so he can take it on his journey?"

"That sounds nice. OK, let's tuck him in."

We gently formed a mound of dirt over the box. "OK, Craigy, place the Popsicle-stick cross above his bed so God knows he's on his way to Heaven."

He grabbed the cross from my hands and shoved it into the ground. "Let's pray for my frog." He patted the ground around Alfie.

As I bowed my head, my son spoke with eloquence and wisdom. I was astonished by his ability to understand so quickly.

"Dear Alfie, you were my best friend. I loved you and so did Mommy. When I go beyond the sunset, I'll find you up there, but don't go too far, OK?" he insisted with a cute lisp. "Amen."

Afterward, we headed inside to bake cookies to lift our spirits. But just as the sweet smell of chocolate chip morsels rose and filled the room, my craving was crushed by a phone call from Mum.

"Jane, the goddamn A/C went out again! I need you to come over. The repairman may take hours, and by then I'll be dead from this heat." Cora dramatically cursed in the background.

Ever since she divorced Smokey, she'd been living on her own. It took countless accusations of cheating before she finally caught him red-handed. Smokey had devoured every bit of her and left without an apology. He wasn't good for her, anyway. But when you're in love, sometimes there are no boundaries to what you'll endure.

She was engulfed with a broken heart—a hell-raising firecracker, jailing herself inside to become a martyr, a victim of her own misery.

"Well, can you come or not?" she scowled over the phone.

"I've got Craigy, Mum, and we just sat down for a snack," I said, picking at the chocolate chips, annoyed by her demands.

"Well, bring your baked goods with you. Besides, I haven't seen that adorable, sweet child for over a month! I'll see you within the hour." She hung up, leaving me with no option.

"Dammit, Cora!" I cursed at the dial tone.

"Dammit, Mommy!" Craig laughed, mimicking me like a sponge.

"No, Craigy, don't copy Mommy!" I sternly looked at him, gathering our things to head out the door.

Bang, Bang, Bang! I felt the wire from her screen door burn my knuckles.

"Cora, I don't have all day!" I shouted.

Before I could pound once again, the door opened, and there stood a nice-looking man to greet us.

"Well, good morning. Cora's in the back if you're looking for her." He smiled as I turned red with embarrassment.

"Sorry for my temper. She drives me nuts sometimes." I tried to keep myself distracted from his intense eyes.

"My mother drives me nuts too. Don't worry about it," he said, winning me over with his Italian accent.

Once Cora spotted Craigy, she softened. "Oh, there he is, my beautiful angel!"

I huffed, blowing the cobwebs off my shoulder. "Well, it looks like you're doing just fine, Mum."

"Better than you, Jane. At least I let people in." She amused herself while pinching Craigy's toes. "So, what do you think?" she hinted, lifting her eyebrows.

"Of what?" I looked around, confused.

"Of Tony! Isn't he a doll?" she whispered under her breath while bouncing my son up and down.

"Mum, you wouldn't!" I angrily pitched a fit.

"Bet your ass I would! Using my A/C was an excuse, and it was the only way to introduce the two of you. So, I'm playing matchmaker. I can't help myself."

She placed Craigy beside some crayons and paper, and our eyes gridlocked as Tony interrupted us.

"Well, everything seems to work just fine, Cora. I checked the A/C, and it has a longer shelf life than you and I combined."

I looked at Cora, raising my eyebrows in agitation. She laughed wickedly, causing my temper to boil.

"Well, that's wonderful. Jane, did you know Tony is a mechanic—and quite handy, should you ever need help?" She winked at the both of us.

"That's great, Mum. But I think all my circuits are working efficiently right now." I grabbed my keys to end the conversation. But Tony quickly chimed in.

"Well, if you ever need anything, anything at all, please give me a call."

"Thank you." I nodded. "Craigy, come on, we need to get going." As I grabbed him, some crayons fell to the floor. "Have a nice day, Mum."

"You too, sweetie. Don't forget to call Tony!" She laughed as I slammed the door shut.

Tony came running after us.

"What do you want?" I said, trying to shrug him off as I struggled to buckle Craigy into his car seat.

"Geez, can't a man offer to help?" He leaned inside to buckle Craig. "Are you always this stubborn?" He grinned, ignoring the sunlight in his eyes.

"Just a little." I stood up to brush myself off.

"Your mother's something else, isn't she?"

"Uh huh, she certainly is."

"Well, listen, I work at the cannery just up the way. Mel's place? Anyhow, if you ever want to grab a drink, come by sometime."

"Does it look like I'm fresh off the press?" I sarcastically looked into his eyes. "I've got a son with allergies and an insane mother. If you'd like to come for dinner, I'll have a bowl of cold soup waiting for you and a slice of bread." I hurried to turn on the ignition.

"Sounds wonderful. What time?" He closed the rear door.

"How's seven?" I replied grinding my teeth, irritated, then revved up the engine.

"What's your address?" he yelled as I got ready to peel off.

"You'll have to get it from my mother!" I yelled back. Pulling away from the curb, I felt as if I'd dodged a bullet.

Lo and behold, he arrived right on time that evening for his soup and bread—and landed right into our hearts. I moved slowly, but Craigy took to him quickly, especially after Tony read him his favorite bedtime stories.

A few nights later, I rested on Tony's shoulder, feeling normal for the first time in years.

"What would make you happy?" His endearing eyes looked into mine.

"That's a loaded question." I tried to sort through what to say next. "I just don't want to run all the time. It's all about Craigy now—the most important thing is stability for him."

Tony grabbed my hands and moved them toward his chest.

"I want to give you that."

And just like that, he dissolved my defenses with his gentleness.

"Why won't you allow me into your world, Jane? Can't I love you?" His words erased my hurt, and our lips finally touched. His brown eyes were tender and saw me without walls.

But in that moment of bliss, I forcefully pushed him away and asked him to leave.

Standing on opposite sides of the screen door, my heart resisted his affection. He was almost too good to be true.

"I apologize. I just can't right now," I said, then turned off the porch light and closed the door.

But hours later, he returned, hollering for me in the wee hours of the morning. Alarmed and half asleep, I answered the door. I could barely catch the light as my eyes adjusted.

"Tony, what on earth are you doing?" I kept my voice low to not wake up Craig.

"I love you!!!" He stumbled from side to side, apparently after a night of drinking. "You mean the world to me! I can't live without you!" He slurred his words while trying to maintain composure.

"Shh! Keep it down! I don't need your problems waking up my little one,"

I said, throwing a tissue box at him before slamming the door.

He called the next morning to apologize, but I was far from amused.

"I'm sorry for acting like an idiot."

"Sorry? You practically broke down my door!"

I scrambled eggs furiously as Craigy looked on, playing with his toy horse.

"I'll make it up to you. Just give me one more chance," he said, embarrassed by his behavior.

"Well, you got to do better than last night. Anyway, I've got to get going. I'm taking care of two of us around here. We'll chat when you're sober."

I should have known better than to trust his judgment in making amends, especially when I caught him carrying a huge pork shoulder from the local butcher up my walkway. He looked like he was getting ready to present a sacrificial lamb.

And then, it happened. My landlord, Emry, who was headed in the same direction, smacked into Tony.

Plunk!

Tony wobbled backward, juggling the pork in his grasp like a circus clown.

"What in God's name?!" my landlord shouted in pain. His eye turned pink upon impact from crashing into the pork.

"Oh, sir, I'm so sorry. Let me help you!" Tony rushed over to press the fleshy rear of the pork against his head to manage the bruising.

"Get that thing away from me! I'm here to talk with Jane, who I've noticed you've been seeing late at night, disturbing the other neighbors. I'm here to evict her and your pork from my property!"

His voice thundered so much that his sparse eyebrows stood straight up.

Locking the door quickly, I peeked through the blinds, praying to God that they'd settle things like grown men.

"Jane, are you in there?" Emry's fist pounded at my door. Tony stood behind him with his thawing pork.

Blindsided by the fiasco, I nervously opened the door, pretending I'd seen nothing.

"Oh, hello, Emry," I casually greeted him. "What seems to be the trouble?"

"Trouble? I've had enough of this nonsense. Your lover here and his pork—along with you and your son—have thirty days to vacate my property!" He shook the papers violently, looking like a pirate with one eye.

But before he could harass me further, his wife appeared from out of nowhere and intervened.

"Emry, you'll do no such thing. She's the cleanest tenant we've ever had!" The landlord's wife fiddled with her curlers. She was a goosy, white-haired woman who always wore a muumuu and found something good in everyone, even piggish men.

Emry looked at her and snarled, then looked back at me. "Thirty days. Am I clear?" Like a wounded playground bully, he felt the lump on his head and patted it.

"Come on, dear. I'll put some ice on it when we get inside." She waddled after him.

After they left, my anger unraveled. I shoved Tony inside and threw the frozen pork across the table.

"Craigy, Mommy needs you to play in your room." I ushered him away.

I closed the door, ready to strangle Tony.

"Well, you did it again! All because of your circus act back there, I have to look for another place to live! Take your pork and get out of here."

Bang, Bang, Bang. The door sounded once more, wearing my patience thin. I screamed.

"Whoever you are, go away!"

"Tony, are you in there? You bastard!"

"Who the hell is that?" My eyes shot toward Tony, trying to make sense of what was happening.

"It's my wife! How did she find out I was here? She must have followed me," Tony ducked down, guilt-stricken and in a panic.

"Your wife? Well, I can't wait to meet her." My sarcasm ran wild as I undid the lock to toss him out.

The introduction was sour, to say the least, as I confronted her face to face. "The son of a bitch is in here. Come get him."

I tugged at Tony's coat, throwing him outside to meet his demise. And, of course, Mr. Emry was standing right between them, perfectly centered with the eviction papers and a prime target for the pork I'd tossed into the air. It knocked him out cold.

"Who the hell are you?" she clenched her jaw.

Suddenly, through the nonsense, I realized a shift in her presence and eyed her slipping a pocketknife back into her purse.

"I'm Tony's wife, Nelly B." She appeared as if wanting to slice me at every angle if she could.

"Take the pork and shove it!" I cursed at Tony.

Nelly gripped her handbag and gave a crooked smile like she was leaving her mark on Tony and me. The glare alone left me fearful.

But I had little time to take it all in. Craigy's crying from the upstairs window took priority.

That evening, neither of us could sleep. I rubbed Vicks on Craig's chest to help soothe his congestion and wiped his tears from exhaustion. Finally, once he became comfortable, I exhaled a sigh of relief that all was quiet. In a deep sleep, he snuggled close to his teddy bear. In those moments it had me wonder what it would be like to live through his eyes, where everything was as beautiful and magical as Alfie, even the soggy Cheerios he'd fool around with in his milk.

My only mission was to keep him safe from the monsters I'd seen as a child, but unfortunately, they had already crept in.

Chapter 16

A Witch at My Door

*"I'd never imagined that I would become a hostage in
my own home. Nelly B's wrath echoed in my mind at night,
taking my dreams for ransom. She'd come riding on a dark broomstick
to engulf the heroes of my world and shape-shift my destiny."*

—JANE CORSARO

Tony's fingertips touched the screen door, as my emotions lay dormant.

"We're getting a divorce." He said, placing his hands in his pockets awaiting my reply. I've been separated for months, but Nelly refuses to accept it. I hope you'll forgive me. It wasn't my intention to hurt you."

Tony looked exhausted but didn't show signs of backing down. "I didn't want to say anything until the divorce was finalized."

Uncertain whether or not to allow him inside, my heart felt tender for him.

Tony proceeded to explain.

"Nelly was never the same after she learned she couldn't bear children. I'm only telling you this, Jane, because I don't want any more secrets," Tony alluded. "I'll find you and Craig another place to live, I promise."

After he resurrected his past, there was an understanding between us. We desired each other's affections, although a sinking feeling crept over me as soon as I allowed him in. It was as if I were allowing something calamitous inside, like a wasp's nest ready to unleash its queen into my bloodstream.

"Tony!" Craigy said, rushing over in his bear-paw pajamas. "Where have you been?" He looked up while chewing on a gummy worm.

"I've been on a pirate's ship, and I've brought you something very special." Tony's eyes twinkled as he handed him a colorful charm that sparkled under the porch light.

"Wow! Look, Mommy!" Craig dangled it in his sticky fingers.

"Come on, little pirate. It's time for bed. Tomorrow we can hunt for treasure." I signaled to Tony.

"Alright, little man, this pirate needs to catch his ship." Tony winked one eye as he kissed me on the forehead.

However, we weren't alone that evening. Nelly's high beams dimmed close by as she stalked us like a hawk. I envisioned her pale face looking in the rear-view mirror as she gripped the steering wheel with jealously, watching our every move.

As time went on, even when we didn't see her, she would always be there. An invisible force always felt.

• • •

A month had come and gone. Tony's divorce was finalized. And, just like he'd promised, he found us a quaint two-bedroom cottage near the edge of town. I remember hanging the first photo on the wall and stepping back to admire my new furnishings.

"Now, don't think you can move in just yet," I smiled cynically, as Tony helped bring in the last few boxes.

He shrugged it off and collected his things, before retiring to get a drink of water.

"Well, if you need anything, I'm right up the street."

I nodded, grateful for his help, and walked him to the door.

"Just give us a little time to adjust." I looked back at Craig giggling at the cartoons.

"I'll be waiting, then." He tilted his hat, making his way outside.

After a couple of weeks, Craig and I finally settled in. I cleaned up the odds and ends until the space felt like home. My little man always kept me busy, entertaining me with his reenactments of the moon landing. He was growing older, and I knew how important it was to have a father figure in his life—more important than my reservations.

"Mommy! Why does everyone in school have two parents?" he shouted over the television.

Careful to find an age-appropriate answer, I closed the fridge and sat down beside him.

"Well, I suppose, not every family is the same," I said, while he remained glued to his favorite show.

"But why can't Tony be my daddy?"

"Oh, honey, don't worry yourself. Mommy's getting to know Tony, and besides, you make Mommy happier than the entire world. Isn't that enough?" I asked, looking into his almond-shaped eyes.

"But I want Tony to live with us!" He puffed his lips. "He's a pirate!" His eyes teared as he chomped on Cheetos, his fingers covered in orange paste.

Oh, how his chubby cheeks left me helpless, as I held him in my arms. And in that moment, I realized something.

"Tony does make us happy, doesn't he?" I asked, impressed by my five-year-old's intuition.

So, without permitting any excuses, I decided to invite Tony over for supper.

"Hello, Tony, this is Jane. I was just talking to my five-year-old who makes more sense than I do these days. Anyway, I would love it if you'd join us for dinner this evening," I said, biting my nails nervously in the background.

"Sure, that sounds great. I'll be over soon."

"Oh, but just one thing—don't bring pork."

Tony and I laughed at our foolish history and immediately after I hung up, the doorbell rang. It startled me so much that I almost caught my apron on fire.

"Be just one second!" I yelled from the kitchen. "Who on earth...?"

I peeked through the peephole and saw Nelly B.

She was hunched forward and staring into the lens. I opened the door but left the chain latched, leaving a slight opening, just enough for me to see half of her face peering inside.

"Is Tony back yet?" Nelly's dry expression made me uncomfortable. She was dressed as if she'd attended a funeral.

"No, Tony's not here. He's staying with Mel up the road," I said, studying her eerie demeanor.

"Well, isn't that nice?" She forced a smile as if it hurt to speak. "If you see him later, please give him this message." She slipped a note into my hand from her pocket.

"I'd feel better if you gave it to him yourself?" I looked up towards the sky, seeing the storm clouds roll overhead. The wind was picking up.

Nelly was a hunter seeking revenge. "You won't want to upset me. Just make sure he gets it." Her eyes gave a sharp warning as the thunder alerted my instincts to comply with her wishes.

Nelly stood in the center of my gravity before I was released from her trance. Slowly, I shut the door, locking the top latch. But when I looked through the peephole the second time, she remained like a voodoo doll, staring blankly at the door before eventually receding.

Soon after I calmed my pulse, the doorbell sounded again, sending my anxiety through the roof. Relieved to see Tony through the curtains, I hurried him inside.

"Oh, thank God it's you! Nelly was here just a moment ago and handed me this note. She said it's urgent. Tony, how does she know where I live?"

He looked frazzled as he reluctantly took the piece of paper from my hand. "She must have followed me."

Dear Tony,
I wanted to let you know that I've adopted a son.
The baby we've always wanted. Please change your mind
and come home. I know you still love me. I can feel it."
Love, Nelly B

Tony's face turned weary as he tossed it in the trash.

"She just doesn't get it!" He slammed his fists on the table, burying his head between his arms. "Nelly's never satisfied. Jane, do me a favor. Whatever you do, just keep your distance if you see her."

But I was already one step ahead of him.

"You don't need to tell me that. There's something odd about her," I said while serving the stew.

With no end in sight, I seemed to become psychic to Nelly's whereabouts. Tony was a reasonable man, but what confused me was when he'd take pity on her and make excuses for her irrational behavior. Her mental instability made me cautious; she had multiple personalities that bordered on insanity. If we ignored her, she'd threaten us with her aggression, or have screaming fits like a toddler. There were no boundaries, as she often showed up uninvited to share her visions of impending death and terrify us with grandiose premonitions.

Once Nelly adopted her son, she hungered even more for Tony's attention. She tried to draw upon on his emotions, especially after the child was diagnosed with a neurological impairment. Her strange invasion of our privacy got worse after Tony and I were married in 1974.

· · ·

Winchester, Virginia, was beautiful during the fall. The leaves surrounded us in a theatrical revival of colors. I swept the leaflets into my hands and tossed them over our heads like fairy dust.

Tony loved being a father. He'd let Craig climb on his back and ride him around the chapel lot. Nevertheless, in my happiest moments, Nelly B was always in the back of my thoughts to tarnish them. Perhaps it was superstition, but deep down, I felt something inhuman was after us. Something sinister.

"I found it!" Tony waved the newspaper as if he'd won the lottery.

"Found what? Sit down and eat your breakfast." I removed the paper from his hands.

"No, really. Look, it's perfect!" He pushed the listing in front of my coffee cup.

Instantly, my eyes filled with happy tears as I nodded in approval. "That's it, isn't it? Our little red home on the hill." My heart felt overwhelmed with joy.

It was more than I'd imagined. And it all became real the moment we pulled up to Highland Drive. It was love at first sight as I soaked in the park with its rolling hillsides. Everything I dreamed of had come true. All it needed was Tony's handy work to bring it back to life. It was a bargain, at only a hundred dollars a month, and would leave us with plenty to grow our family. Surrounding the two-story Colonial was a forest of trees, and across the street was an old church lined with rose bushes fit for a queen.

Tony handed me the keys, and I unlocked the front door. I took in that precious moment and pictured Craig's older years growing up there and the memories that would remain forever.

The house had floor-to-ceiling wallpaper, a simple kitchen, and was full of charm. Better yet, it had the security and the freedom I'd always wanted—and Mum wasn't far away. She was getting older and had suffered complications from osteoporosis, which caused immense pain. Still, all it took was a shot of whiskey to get her to calm down whenever I bathed her. Somehow, she still had the stamina to speak her mind and curse like the dickens after I fought her tooth and nail. But sadly, I was all Mum had nearby to care for her, so she reluctantly compromised.

"Tony, will you answer the telephone? I'm knee-deep out here," I shouted from the garden just before washing my hands with the hose.

"Hello," he said, distracted by the television. Knocking on the window, he mouthed to me, "It's Nelly," and held up the receiver, so I rushed inside. "We're doing fine, Nelly. How can I help you?"

"I'm sorry to disturb you, but I've got this problem with my sink. Could you come take a look at it?" Clearly, she was trying to coerce him into her web.

Tony was reluctant to respond.

"What time?"

"Anytime. You know where I am."

"OK, I'll be over after dinner."

Immediately, I waged a fit.

"What is it with that woman? It's like she can't leave us alone."

"Jane, give her a little leeway. She needs our help occasionally." He kissed my forehead to assure me Nelly wasn't going to cause any trouble.

"For Christ's sake, Tony, really? If she's not calling for repair work, she's calling us because she's dying from an overdose."

Tony stopped me and placed his hands on my shoulders. "I feel sorry for her. Let's try and practice what we preach, honey. I promise I won't be gone too long."

"OK, have it your way. But just let me be clear—if you ever decide to pack your clothes and go to her, don't ever think of coming back," I said, shooting him a stern look.

Nelly B wasn't about to give up on my family. The harder she spun her web, the more he got reeled in, like a fly gasping for air.

That evening, after Tony returned, we made love. We had surrendered to her addiction and promised ourselves we'd ignore her fabrications while navigating our own lives. When the sun rose the next morning, I slipped under his arms to confess what I'd been thinking for a long time.

"I want Craig to have a brother." I snuggled on top of him, kissing his chin.

"Well, I think that's wonderful, but what about your health? Didn't your doctor mention the risks?" he said, trying not to upset me.

"I've made another appointment with the doctor. I'm not ready to give up just yet."

• • •

The following week I was at my doctor's office.

"Considering the complications that could arise, Jane, I really don't think this would be in the best interest of you or your unborn baby. The chances of you dying are likely. Please heed my warning before you decide to get pregnant." My doctor's eyes strained as I sat up on his examination table.

Angry and unwilling to reason, I spoke up.

"Well, I guess I'll take a chance now, won't I?"

"Jane, I'm just giving proper medical advice. Statistically, you and your baby will die."

"Doctor, are you a man of faith?"

"Well, of course, I am." His eyebrows narrowed.

"Well, if you are, then you should believe in miracles. And one more thing—get your head out of the books and ask the Lord if he gives a shit about your statistics!"

• • •

On the drive home, I understood what the doc was trying to tell me, but my desire to have another baby and a sibling for Craig overruled his warning.

Tony was concerned—as he should have been. But in the pit of my stomach, I knew I'd survive. I had already undergone the throes of tragedy and dealt with the wicked witch at my door. God had another coin toss for me. A few weeks later, I found out Tony and I were pregnant.

Chapter 17

Evil Walks In

*"I can still remember watching those vibrant sunsets,
sitting close to my mother and baby boy. We'd find refuge
on those rolling hillsides. In our own wakeful silence,
the serenity lay between us. God had carried us home."*

—JANE CORSARO

A few months into my pregnancy, my body appeared to be managing the stress and changes I was undergoing day by day. Also, there was a rumor circulating that Nelly was dating again, which kept her away from Tony and less preoccupied with our lives.

The summer had surrendered into the hands of fall, and the colder months were unfolding as I neared my midterm.

When the weather was tolerable, I'd take Craig and my mother to Round Hill Park. The lush fields of greenery and fall foliage were surrounded by mature trees and white picket fences. There were even rolling hillsides, perfect to sit on and watch the sky perform its magic.

Our eyes were immersed in wonder. We watched as the light would fade beyond the horizon's lids, sinking into night. Autumn purified the air with the earthiness of tree bark, cloves, and winter's breath. It was a place that lifted our spirits.

• • •

Thanksgiving was finally here, the trimmings and harvest set abundantly on the table. Mum would join us that evening. Although her health was declining rapidly, she wouldn't pass up the holidays. Wheelchair-bound, she enjoyed watching us entertain one another.

The blistering cold outside rattled the windowpanes while we kept warm indoors. Craig had the honor of cutting the turkey and was becoming a bright young man, exceeding a higher-than-average IQ of 135. He could see past the veil of life, deeper than I ever could, which fueled his perceptions of others and his surroundings. Strangers admired him for his generous nature and endearing softness, and the world was his canvas.

After washing up in the kitchen and gathering the plates after supper, Tony snuck me a kiss and told me how beautiful I was, though I felt like a round bowling ball.

Later that night, when everyone was fast asleep, I curled up beside the window frame, watching the snow cascade down like cotton. The chimes of the grandfather clock lulled me to sleep in a house with all the people I cherished.

Overnight, the town was blanketed in snow, and in the morning, our chimney's smoke danced through woodland forests and above our wintry wonderland. It carried us all the way through the holiday season. And even when Christmas had come and gone, the spirit of the holidays left me whole.

I reminisced how Craig had rushed to the Christmas tree and cherished his presents, ripping through the wrapping paper and crying out with excitement when he saw his wooden toy train or paper airplane. It was the simple things in life that made us a family. We had little, and yet, we had it all.

I was proud of our tiny tree that made wrapping the few gifts that we had worthwhile. The holiday bedtime stories I read Craig when he was young made him a believer in Old St. Nick. We'd always search for him on Christmas Eve, looking up at the starry night sky, pointing at shooting stars.

The magic of what the holidays represented during my era was the communal spirit and praise as each neighbor took pride in their outdoor decorations and retailers adorned their shops with twinkling lights and mystical figurines. It was a time I'll always cherish. A simpler time, before men's hearts became unclean with pride, greed, and the lust for immense gain and power.

I saw my town fall apart as I grew older. It was as if the spirit of all we knew was no longer good enough. Humankind always wants more than it needs. Like an incurable virus within ourselves, we will become our own destruction.

• • •

Coming up on nine months, it was almost time for my delivery. As busy as I'd become making arrangements, in the back of my mind, I couldn't forget my doctor's warning. Still, Tony soothed me with his reassurance and loving intimacy. I tried hard to focus on the positive, ignoring the uncertainty of my body going into labor and the sacrifice it would make for me to bear another child.

• • •

The fireworks boomed overhead, lighting up the night sky on New Year's Eve, only weeks from my delivery date. Right as the countdown was over, I felt an intense pain strike my lower abdomen like a knife, but it quickly went away making me shrug it off and carry on.

However, in the final days of January, I knew something was terribly wrong. I grabbed the lower part of my belly and straightened up, only to hunch over in excruciating pain.

"Tony!" I screamed as my breath escaped me. "Tony! Something's wrong!" I barreled over in agony, alerting Craig, who immediately led me to the couch.

The discomfort continued to increase, surging down my lower extremities. It was like powerful razor blades cutting through my insides. I reached under my dress to place pressure where the blood was escaping and dripping onto the carpet.

Tony rushed to call an ambulance, his eyes wide with terror. "My wife needs medical care! Please! She's bleeding and pregnant! Hurry!"

Craig raced to grab towels to soak up the blood. My body was going into shock as the pressure intensified. And that's when I knew I needed to clench every muscle to seize from pushing because I knew I would rupture and die.

As I heard the sirens approach, I kept going in and out of consciousness, but I was aware Tony remained at my side, trying to keep me alert.

"Come on, stay awake, Jane! Don't you give up on us!"

We were separated at the ICU, where I was in God's hands now.

Back in surgery, my unborn child and I fought the battle of our lives as the doctors worked tirelessly. That is when I felt God's presence move through me. It was a potency of unconditional love I'd never known before. I was saved by His grace, and we survived when all odds were against us. After a harrowing cesarean surgery, Dean Anthony was born January 31, 1977.

Tony rushed to my side, overcome with emotion as he cradled his son. I'll never know the horrors he lived through during those couple of hours, but God had worked another miracle in my life. My family was complete.

• • •

At home, Craig looked mesmerized, admiring his kid brother's perfection. He ran his hands down Dean's legs adoringly and became his protector from that day forward.

"He squeals a lot." Craig laughed, tickling the bottoms of Dean's feet.

"That's what you did when you were his age."

Craig immediately took to his new role. "I'm going to show him everything. How to build model cars, play with paper airplanes, and run as fast as me!"

"I know, honey. Dean will have the best big brother in the entire world."

Recovering from surgery wasn't easy, especially not back in those days. I was on bed rest for some time, so naturally, Craig and Tony helped around the house until I could regain my strength. Mum also checked in daily. She knew about my near-death experience in the hospital but couldn't be there because of her condition.

"So, you survived another hell storm?" her voice struggled to project.

"I know. Can you believe it?" My heart became heavy hearing her voice lose its strength.

"Jane, you always were a fighter. I guess we have to thank the hot peppers I ate when I was pregnant with you." She sighed.

"Get some sleep, Mum. We'll talk later this week."

Eventually, my strength returned—but sadly, Mum's never would. In the depths of my imagination, I'd paint her and me as one person. She was a woman of dominance connected to a strong-willed child. If we'd have looked in the mirror, I believe we would have seen each half made whole by the other, not broken.

Glowing from motherhood, I headed toward the kitchen, rocking Dean in my arms. I placed him in his bassinet that was on the countertop and took notice of Craig building an obstacle maze in the front yard. Amused by his brilliance, I watched him turn nature into art.

It was nearing five o'clock, and Tony would be home soon. I began to clean up and get things ready to start dinner. I washed the morning dishes and placed them on the dish rack while reaching back to rock Dean, who was drooling with each giggle.

"Mommy is going to tickle the little baby boy." I playfully crept closer to Dean as his chubby feet kicked vigorously at my funny faces.

"One. Two—"

"Three!" a voice shouted from behind me.

I could feel someone's nimble fingers touch my hips, their breath raising the hairs on my neck. A danger invaded me.

"Nelly!" I swallowed in astonishment. "How did you get in here?"

She slithered toward us and looked emotionless as if peering deep into my soul.

"The door was open, so I let myself in."

Instinctively, I drew closer to Dean, fearing she'd harm us. After all, she had walked in without being invited.

"Haha! Hahaha!" She cackled as she shook her finger in my face with a menacing evil. Like a rolling thunder, I could feel her rage build and sensed her placing a malevolent curse on our home.

Nelly was no longer Nelly B. She was a satanic replica of demonic proportions. Evil walked inside my home that day—and if I'd had holy water, I would've drunk it.

Looking at Nelly was like looking into the mind of a wild animal. Her stare was repulsive. She continued to laugh, scorning me with pleasure.

Dean started to cry, alerting Craig to rush inside. I backed into a corner.

"Mommy, the clouds are coming in!" He pointed toward the window.

Realizing the horror of Nelly in my kitchen, I decided to play the actress to protect us.

"Nelly, I've got to get back to making dinner. I'm a mess, as you can see. Let's catch up later." I composed myself … but all the while, Nelly's eyes surveyed her surroundings like a snake.

She peered down at Dean, then walked past Craig, running her nails over the top of his head. "I'll be seeing you all again soon." She shot an eerie look before fading from the parlor entryway.

Craig latched onto me tightly. "What's wrong with her, Mommy?"

"Nothing, honey. Nelly was just stopping by." I looked out the front door that she'd left open.

Within minutes, the sky was covered in clouds, just as Craig expected.

• • •

"What's got into you?" Tony said, trying to stop me as I shoved past him.

"I'll be back in a minute." I hurried to grab my coat. "I'm heading to my mother's!"

"What's going on, Jane?"

"Your ex-wife came by this afternoon." I zipped up my raincoat. "Something's not right with her, Tony. I'll be back soon," I said, running out into the pouring rain to start the car.

As I drove recklessly, I couldn't help but replay the afternoon's confrontation with Nelly. My mind couldn't erase her insidious laugh through the rain coming down in sheets.

I barged into my mum's. "We need to talk!"

"What's wrong, Jane?" she said, setting aside her book.

"Nelly B. She came into my house today unannounced and frightened me and the children. Something isn't right with that woman. I think she wants to hurt us!"

"Jane, calm down," she insisted, grabbing my arm.

"She wants me—" I said faintly.

Mother had realized the situation even before I had. "Jane, you have something she doesn't have. Therefore, her pain must be projected onto you and your family. It's a bitter pill she must swallow, my dear— the sin of jealousy."

"Well, what should I do?"

"Keep your enemies close," she said. "This Nelly lady has a mission, but you'll get around it." She sipped her coffee and rested back on her pillow.

When I left Mum that evening, I felt determined to do whatever was necessary to defend my family and keep Nelly away. After I made it home, I placed my coat down and rummaged through the mail, hearing Tony bathe Dean in the distance.

Even though I was inside, it didn't feel like home anymore. It felt tainted after Nelly unleashed her mark on my walls. The dark magic turned its ugly face and engraved its curse around every corridor. If only the walls could speak. Nelly's Black Mass covered us with blood as thick as her envy. I could sense it. I could taste it. Her spell was far more real than any fairytale I'd ever believed as a child. Hers was a real poison to our lives, a horrible plague cast upon us that couldn't be seen or touched.

Evil had walked inside that day. To know evil is to look it in the eyes.

"Nelly B, what have you done?" I whispered to myself, shutting the bedroom door.

Chapter 18

BATTLESHIPS AND BROOMSTICKS

*"Somedays I'd become Grace Kelly, Bette Davis, or even Joan Crawford.
But eventually, I'd become Boris Karloff. It was one of the many
alter egos I'd mastered to outwit the devils of the world
and outsmart the one woman who wanted to cause harm.
She was guided by a force that was hungry for us."*

—JANE CORSARO

Dean was a rambunctious child who imagined he was a handyman like his father. His cheeky smile lit up his face as he carried Tony's tools around, wobbling to hold himself up. For most of the day, he'd tap at the outside cement, scrape, and play with sticks.

The sparrows would come and go as he'd loudly hammer away. But they'd always make their way back to perch high on the treetops to wait for their time to land.

Dean's world was full of exploration, which made me keep a strong eye on him, fearing that Nelly would come and take him from me. There wasn't a day that went by that I didn't check the locks on the doors when Tony was away, sometimes checking them twice to make sure each latch was fastened properly. It was unfortunate because no one locked their doors in my neighborhood. But I had to.

I felt like a child all over again, targeted for something I didn't deserve but had to endure. Suddenly, a panic attack rushed over me; that's when I heard the school children laughing in the well of my memory and saw their wicked stares as they kicked dirt in my face. I could hear Chuck's husky voice demoralizing me and saw the stern face of my mother in the darkness, drawn in blood. My life was playing tricks all over again. I banished myself to the back room, hiding from the monsters in my mind.

My anxiety made it hard for me to breathe, making it feel like my lungs were drained of oxygen. From afar, I heard the ambient clanging of Dean's toy trucks—louder and louder as I spiraled out of control. Doom, shame, and fear set in at once like a calamity. I paced back and forth, turning in circles, again, barely able to hold my sanity intact as the harbingers of the future surrounded me. The sounds from the outside world rippled through the blinds. I covered my ears. Death felt like it would engulf my body, like a tidal wave of terror. I collapsed to the ground, bracing my soul for restitution.

These episodes brought back the giants that couldn't be ignored in the murky crevices of my torment. I wept into the carpet to dislodge my mind.

After a deep cry that appeared out of nowhere, I pulled myself up onto the bed sheets and breathed more steadily, exhausted from my racing thoughts. Almost immediately, the pounding in my chest subsided. The habitual beating had ended. Once I was calm, I washed up and grabbed onto the sides of the sink, bearing all my weight as I stared into the mirror. My eyes were heavy from lack of rest. I was a survivor. I'd always been. But when you're living in the fast lane—how I had lived— you have little time to feel, connect, or respond to your own suffering.

"Honey, where are you?" I heard Tony's voice as he opened the front door.

"I'm back here. Be out in a minute," I said, brushing my hair and pinching under my eyes to erase the swelling.

"I was just in the bathroom. How was your day?" I asked, walking out to greet him.

"It was fine." He looked at me, concerned, and then turned to Dean. "How's my big man?" He lifted him into his arms. Dean giggled and patted both his hands on Tony's cheeks and wiggled out of his arms to continue playing.

"Anything?" Tony asked.

"No, she hasn't been by in a few days." I looked away to hide my face.

Craig was just returning from school.

"Hello, honey, how was your day?"

"Good, I have a ton of homework—we're learning about space!" He lugged his backpack to his bedroom.

"That's great, sweetie! Supper will be ready soon."

Tony played with a few loose strands of hair and placed them behind my ear. "You sure you're, OK?"

"Yes, I'm fine." I shrugged it off.

During dinner, Craig could sense something was on my mind as I picked at the meatloaf on my plate. "Have you seen the witch today?"

"Craig, I told you not to mention her anymore." I spooned some mashed potatoes into my mouth.

"Your mother's right. It's not nice to call people names. Besides, I'd rather hear about your schoolwork."

"Well, I don't like her," Craig fussed, pushing the plate away and excusing himself from the table.

Moments later, the phone rang.

"I'll get it." Tony wiped his face and placed the napkin on the table.

"Hello?" He looked over at me to ensure I was all right. "Calm down, Nelly! What's the matter?"

I could hear her hysterically screaming through the phone. "What have I done to my eyes!? I've gone blind!"

"Alright, just hang on, I'll be right over!" He immediately hung up the phone and fled towards the door.

"She's playing make-believe again, isn't she? One minute she's sick; the next minute she's dying. When in God's name will you listen to me?" I said, grabbing his coat to keep him from leaving.

"I know what you're thinking, Jane, but I don't think she's crying wolf this time. I'll be back in a moment."

That evening I waited, imagining Nelly's performance in my head.

• • •

I wasn't there, but this was how Tony explained it.

Pulling up the uneven driveway, Tony had no choice but to park near the overgrown shrubs swallowing the property. When he approached, the porch was infested with dead bugs and cobwebs, making it difficult to see through the windows. He kept banging on the door and calling Nelly's name but with no success. Finally, a malnourished figure opened the door, peering out as if to see the light for the first time. It was Leonard—Nelly's adopted son.

Once inside, Tony noticed trash strewn throughout the house and demanded to know what was going on as he covered his nose from the stench.

Leonard spoke slowly.

"Shhh. Mother's uneasy right now. Shadows tell her things." With a nervous twitch, Leonard spoke in short sentences.

"Shadows?" Tony asked him.

Right about then, an icy chill made its way past the heavy curtains that partitioned the living room. Everything had been shuffled around, different than what he remembered. Things were turned upside down and hoarded to the ceilings, covering the windows from even a shred of sunlight.

Tucked away, Tony spotted Nelly hunched over her writing desk. He could see dead rodents next to piles of debris which instantly made him nauseous and hesitant to approach.

Nelly sniffled.

"I'm sorry you have to see me this way, but I had this terrible nightmare."

"What do you mean?" Tony moved in closer to examine her.

"I dreamed I went blind." The chair creaked as she slowly turned around and raised her forehead as if she were possessed.

"I don't understand, Nelly! What games are you playing with my family?" Tony hollered.

Startled, Leonard covered his ears, humming to tune out the noise and soothe himself.

After that point, Tony said the atmosphere of the room spiraled downwards. Nelly slammed her pen against the wood and snarled at Tony.

"I am sick and tired of having to justify myself to you! That bitch took you from me! And now what's fair is fair." She sunk lower in tone, as if a growl escaped from her throat, alerting Tony to something unworldly present.

Nelly wiped her face with a soiled dish rag, smudging her eyeliner into her premature wrinkles.

"I won't allow her to separate us! I'm sorry, but I can't stop it—it's coming, Tony. I've seen it."

She let out an agonizing cry on the edge of laughter. "It's coming." Nelly stood up and walked past Tony as if he were a ghost.

Frightened by her behavior, Tony demanded answers. "What the hell are you talking about, Nelly!?"

But she was unresponsive.

Terrorized by her split personality, Tony collected his things and made his way out.

On the drive home, he was in denial that Nelly was capable of harm—believing that the occult and black magic were just superstition. He didn't want to admit it, but what he was dealing with was something more than just Nelly.

• • •

A week later she came by to apologize. She blamed it on the medication and its side effects, but I wasn't buying it.

"I wanted to come over and apologize for my poor behavior. I have no business interrupting your lives. I hope you will forgive me." She nervously picked at her fingernails.

"We appreciate your apology, Nelly," I said, trying to remain confident in her sincerity.

Nelly looked around and sighed with relief.

"Well, before I leave, would it be all right if I take some pictures of your garden? You always take such good care of it."

"Alright," I agreed, just as Tony was finishing up with the children outside.

"You have such an impeccable home, Jane. It's fantastic, really. I'll just take a few pictures and be on my way," she assured me, making her way down the steps.

But as I watched from the window, I noticed that her camera was pointing toward my car and then at my children.

I quickly turned off the sink and crossed her outside.

"I thought you were taking pictures of the garden, Nelly?" I scolded her while restraining my anger.

"Oh, I did take a few, but I just noticed your new car." She smiled over at the children. "They're beautiful boys. I hope you don't mind that

I took a few pictures of them as well. Tony must be so happy." She gathered her bag from the ground like a calm criminal trying to make a run for it. "Have a nice day!" She waved from her car window, passing us by in the haze of the summer heat.

I looked on as her engine's smoke blinded me. I shooed it away from my face.

"Did she get what she needed?" Tony looked on, squinting his eyes.

"Nope, she'll be back for another round," I said, preparing my soul for battle.

• • •

My mind hunted around that evening. I shuffled through the years of mementos that I'd kept tucked away, searching for something, but I didn't know exactly what I was looking for.

Then I remembered the traveling woman that I'd met as a teenager. She magically appeared in my mind, and I remembered her stark warning: *"You must beware of a light-haired woman who will enter your life. Do not befriend her—she is treacherous!"*

I remembered the urgency in her voice as she scanned my hands like they were a road map of my destiny. How could I have forgotten? A lump formed in my throat. "Nelly B was that woman!" I gasped.

Before I retired to bed that evening, I swept my outside porch in deep meditation. The coarse bristles of the broomstick carried the dirt onto the dustpan. When I was finished, I held the broomstick's neck stoically, looking out at the horizon as the sun's splendor melted away. The battle had only just begun.

Chapter 19

DEADLY NIGHTSHADE

*"The nightshade in my neighbor's garden mirrored
Nelly's poisonous appetite. She was skillful in planting her seeds
in my life, like Rumpelstiltskin spinning gold thread around
my husband and children. Only this time, her spell had worked."*

— JANE CORSARO

My family was my life, and I'd do anything for them. My boys continued to grow into bright young men, and although my home was full
of horseplay and unforgiving bruises, I cherished every minute of it. It
was another cycle of life reborn, with all the challenges and triumphs I
could handle.

But it was the hurdles that God gave me that made me fight harder
and led me to grace. What doesn't kill us makes us stronger.

• • •

"You're in perfect health!" The optometrist finished checking my pupils,
waving his bright light back and forth.

"Well, that's great!" I said, opening and closing my eyes to readjust to the light.

"Keep up the excellent work, and we'll see you back here in a year." He gestured me out the doorway.

On my way home, I decided to pass by my old neighborhood just across the river and was comforted to see that Brick Alley wasn't lined with brothels anymore. In fact, the streets were wiped clean of trash, and new storefronts were being put up. Times were changing, and change was inspiring.

The air smelled fresher. Even the lakes glistened with new illumination, and the Pennsylvania sky I knew as a child was cleaner than ever before. I could see lush landscapes again, vast valleys, and old farms lining the winding roads. The mill's thick smoke had faded away, leaving a beautiful portrait, perfect for an artist to capture.

It felt freeing to drive along the highs and lows of the back roads. Just below, the beasts of the river clashed, but high above, the wispy winds carried me away to the promised land everyone dreamed of.

In the distance, I noticed a rainbow emerging from the afternoon rains. God's colors shone vividly over the landscape. It made me wonder how God loved us so much, even after we butchered his creation. His heart must have been broken many times, but I was told his mercy was great. The Lord continued to bless me with biblical insight as I pulled up to the curb.

"What took you so long?" Tony greeted me at the doorstep.

"Oh, nothing. I just thought I'd take a drive today and enjoy the hillsides. My eye doctor said my eyesight is perfect!" I slapped his backside and kissed his cheek.

"That's great, honey!" he said, following me to the kitchen, gesturing quietly toward the living room.

"When you get a chance, I think our young man may have a crush at school. Her name is Andrea," he whispered. "I overheard him talking to her today."

My heart suddenly felt heavy. I was delighted but heartsick that my boy was becoming a man. He was only a teenager and still wearing braces, but I was softened to know his heart was expanding.

"Hi, sweetie. How was your day today?" I said, resting beside him.

"Hi, Mum." Craig continued to focus on his studies.

"Well, how are you?" I smoothed out his hair, kissing him on the forehead. "A little bird told me you have a new friend named Andrea?" I pushed his chin up so he'd look at me with those adoring eyes.

"How do you know about Andrea?" His face turned a bright red. "Dad!" he yelled, annoyed by his eavesdropping.

"Oh, honey, it's fine. It's OK if you like her," I said, trying to ease his worry.

"Well, she's all right." He rolled his eyes, still bright red with embarrassment.

"Is she pretty?"

"Kind of." Craig circled the pen on his writing pad, clearly distracted, yet still trying to concentrate.

"Well, I'm happy for you, Craigy," I said, ready to leave his bedroom.

"Mum, can you not call me Craigy?" He looked at me mortified.

"OK, Craig."

I shut the door and took a deep breath.

"Mommy!" Dean's voice trailed over the entire house.

"What is it, baby?" I asked. He gestured toward the window, then stuck his thumb in his mouth.

Outside, I could see Nelly parking near the curb. She emerged carrying an obscene number of gifts as if it were Christmas.

"Knock, knock," she delighted. "I just thought I'd drop by since I was in the neighborhood and give Dean and Craig some presents," she said, struggling to keep her balance.

"What's the occasion?" I asked as I let her inside.

"Oh, nothing in particular. I just wanted to do something nice for your boys." She caught her breath as she made her way straight for Dean, pouring everything onto the table. As soon as she had her hands free, her tone changed. Craig joined us at the table. She walked calmly toward him and dropped a quarter in front of his textbook. It spun in circles until Craig's palm flattened it.

Nelly B's demeanor quickly shifted to a dull and serious undertone. "Save this for something special."

"A quarter?" Craig looked confused. "Thanks?" He looked up at her icy gaze.

"OK, well, you all have a good night! I have to head home and get cooking." She turned, busying herself with her purse, and walked out the door like she had won the lottery.

That wasn't the first time Nelly made up excuses to come and go, leaving behind odd gifts for the boys. I knew she wanted Dean and Tony to herself and was trying to get rid of me and Craig—and she always seemed to be ten steps ahead of us.

The next day, I dropped Craig off at school. "Have a nice day, sweetie!" I leaned out the car window and waved goodbye.

"Bye, Mum!" He waved before quickly becoming distracted by Andrea, his new crush.

It was the first time I'd seen her. Immediately, she took my breath away. She had exquisite South Asian features, long wavy black hair, pale brown eyes, and a smile that could light up a room.

My motherly eyes could see how my son had become infatuated with her. But I learned that it wasn't just her good looks that enticed him; it was also her high IQ and ability to keep Craig challenged when they'd compete in honors classes.

I rolled up the passenger window and watched Dean in the rearview mirror making funny faces as he imitated the two love birds.

"Now don't you get old like your brother!" I playfully tugged his leg as I pulled away from the curb.

· · ·

Craig had lost his boyish features overnight and had become a handsome young man. As Craig and Andrea became more serious in the years that followed, I learned much more about the young woman who had captivated my son's heart. Andrea came from a strict Indian family. Her father was a professor, and her mother was a respected nurse. Both parents disapproved of Craig and Andrea's dating, perhaps due to different customs. But somehow, they remained inseparable and tore down borders just to be together. Like Romeo and Juliet, they overcame adversity, even if it meant going against her parents' wishes.

"Your son is gifted, Mrs. Corsaro. Craig's IQ is well above average. Have you ever considered placing him in our advanced honors program? It will likely guarantee his acceptance into some of the finest colleges our country has to offer," his high school teacher stated, flashing a confident smile at Tony and me.

"Well, we haven't really discussed it as a family. I'll talk it over with Craig this weekend." I smiled and patted Tony's leg to follow my lead.

"Thank you both for meeting with me today. I know it will be a lot more work, pressure, and responsibility, but your son has excellent potential." He grinned as he opened his office door and led us out.

Yes, Craig had a natural gift. From the time he was born, he had a developed intelligence, but my son was extremely sensitive and overcome with empathy for the world's troubles. I was concerned with the pressure he had of being an overachiever and what that would do to his heart in the long run.

"You don't think I can do it?" Craig looked at me with a defeated look on his face.

"That's not what I'm saying at all. You're already excelling in your classes. This might just be too much all at once. And besides, you have Andrea in your life—"

"Andrea has nothing to do with this! This is about my future—not hers!" He tossed his books off his bed and stomped out of the room.

Later that evening, I apologized for overstepping my boundaries.

"I want to enroll in this program, and I hope you'll both support me," Craig said without reservation.

"If that's what you want, your mother and I will support you," Tony gave his blessing after seeing my nod of approval.

Craig's eyes filled with appreciation.

"You're going to be fine, astronaut." I looked back to congratulate him.

• • •

During the floods, the unforgiving storms, and muggy summers, our little red house weathered Mother Nature's wrath, and we all survived it.

Every weekend, it appeared that Tony would be on the roof, spouting obscenities while trying to repair holes caused by some force of nature. His hands were as rough as tree bark, ashy and callused from years of hard labor, just like my father's, but he was determined to keep things in place.

Tony cleaned up well when he showered, rinsing away the residue of his labors, and we'd still find time to sneak away to rekindle our romance. Thankfully, when Mum felt strong enough, she'd watch Dean, allowing Tony and me to escape to the movies or park and look over the city below, making out like teenagers in the back seat.

When Mum's doctors told me she'd only have a few years to live, the only thing left to do was forgive her, just like I had with Father. Her roots were part of mine. Her DNA was the yin and yang of my design.

• • •

When the seasons allowed us to take small family trips, Dean and Craig would race to the car, practically tripping over each other in a frenzy to see who could get there first.

This time, though, we were in for a shock. The vehicle windows were bashed in, vandalized beyond repair. Glass was shattered all over the street, leaving little to be salvaged.

The boys and I yelled for Tony while Craig circled the car to investigate the debris. Tony ran out, fuming from the ears and shouting. He frantically assessed the damage. "What son of bitch would do this!?"

I lifted my head, surveying the neighborhood's untouched parked cars. There was no sign of burglary or vandalism nearby. None whatsoever. But as I drew closer to the passenger window, I noticed a few quarters on the passenger floor. Craig always carried pocket change with him, even saving the quarters from Nelly's uninvited visits—but he never sat in the passenger seat.

Apparently, it was her that had paid us another visit.

Later that evening, we had to shut our doors due to an argument.

"For God's sake, why do you always blame Nelly!?" Tony shouted.

"Because she's obsessed with you, Tony. Don't you see it!? Nelly B has created nothing but problems ever since we let her into our lives!"

"Jane, she's apologized over and over again. What more do you need from her?" he said naïvely and tossed his clothes to one side of the bed.

"That's just it. You don't think she's capable of harm, but she is! Nelly B hates me—admit it, Tony. She can't stand the fact that you and I had Dean, and all she's interested in is a family with you! She wants me and Craig out of the picture, and she'll stop at nothing to make that a reality," I said, yanking back the covers before climbing into bed.

"I've known her a lot longer than you have, Jane. She was my wife for many years. Don't you think I would protect you if I thought for a minute she would harm any of us?"

"If she's so innocent, why has she been hanging around here for so long? The woman can't even hold a relationship for more than a few weeks before she's back on our doorstep looking for you! She wants you, Tony," I screamed, throwing the sheets off the bed and walking out of the bedroom.

"What's wrong, Mum?" I felt Craig pull my arm.

"Nothing, honey." I cupped his face, trying to disguise my worry.

"I know why you're scared." Craig paused, apprehensive to share more. "I've seen Nelly's vehicle pull up around here after midnight when you're both asleep. I didn't want to say anything because I never saw her cross the garden, but she stands there, sometimes over an hour," he said.

Right after Craig confirmed all my fears, I went to check on Dean, who was sleeping soundly. From his room, I looked out onto the street, observing each amber streetlight as I tried to shake my panic.

Then, mysteriously, I saw a figure appear in the shadows of the silver moon. Was my mind playing tricks on me—or was that Nelly standing across the street by a row of deadly nightshade? I squinted to make her out, but her figure seemed to waver in and out like an illusion tricking my mind.

The deadly nightshade bloomed with deceit, invading the garden with its poisonous berries that could kill you as soon as they touched your lips. I shut my eyes and opened them, terrified she'd see me. Thankfully, that night, it was only a figment of my imagination. However, she would find me the next morning, as if she could sense she was in my thoughts.

• • •

With the boys at school and Tony at work, I folded the last piece of laundry. I went to head outside, but just before, I checked the peep-hole—only to be startled by Nelly's eyes staring into mine. I opened the door with a swift jerk.

"Well, hello, Nelly. To what do I owe the pleasure?" I asked, ready to bury her in mud.

"I was in the neighborhood and wanted to see if Tony was here?" She looked past my shoulders as if anxiously waiting for him to appear.

"He's not here right now. He'll be home later."

"Oh, isn't that a shame? I wanted to tell him the good news!" She triumphed past me, carrying a large piece of clothing toward the kitchen.

"Just look at this dress. Can you believe this used to fit me? I've got to tell you … I've lost so much weight in the past few months … he probably won't even recognize me!" She seemed to embrace her own deception.

Nelly unfolded the extra-large dress—three times her size—onto my counter, trying to fool me. Only thing is, I knew that Nelly had never fit the size of the garment she was holding. In fact, she was the same size she'd always been. Feeling uneasy, I went to pour some coffee.

"Well, I'll definitely let Tony know," I said, refraining from making eye contact. But in a rare instant of testing her, I asked, "Are you sure this was yours?" I lifted the dress to look at the aged floral print.

"Well, of course, it was! What is it with you, Jane? I come by excited to tell you the good news, and you play down my sincerity." She rose abruptly. "You know the problem with women like you? You're too goddamn jealous! Did it ever occur to you that I may be thinner than you are—and that Tony is still in love with me?" She paused, forcing me to acknowledge her insanity.

"No, Nelly, that's not what I'm implying." I stared back at her, try-ing not to stutter. "I think you'd better go now." I stood my ground and reached behind me to grab a kitchen knife just in case she charged me.

"That's fine. I'll leave…for now," Nelly said, brushing past me. But then she stopped midway. "Do you remember the time I thought I went blind? Turns out it was just a hallucination. I'm sure you know what that is?" Nelly rambled on. "But do you know what's even spookier? I saw something was coming after you, Jane." She contained herself, saying no more, then gave me an ungodly grin. "Well, have a lovely day."

Later that afternoon, I didn't mention my encounter to Tony. I made dinner, as usual, said goodnight to the boys, and lay back in bed, reading a book to tune her out.

But it had been an exhausting encounter, and reading only made my eyes fuzzy. After a few paragraphs, I decided it was best to rest.

That next morning, my eyes still felt cloudy. I washed up and scrubbed twice, throwing ice-cold water on my eyes, until my vision returned to normal. We hurried through breakfast, and before I knew it, I was dropping Dean and Craig off at school.

"Have a nice day, sweetie!" I waved to Dean, watching him join his friends.

"Bye, Mum!" he shouted back.

As I pulled out of the schoolyard, my mind was filled with thoughts of the cereal mess and burnt toast I had to clean up. My senses were amplified. I heard children singing as they crossed the crosswalk, saw the bright colors of the streetlights flicker, and inhaled the sweet aroma coming from the local bakery. It was like any normal day as I drove on the outskirts of town.

Normal, that is, until a burning sensation scorched my eyes. The road blurred. I rubbed my eyelids vigorously, thinking I was suffering from an allergic reaction. But the more I rubbed, the more irritated they became. That's when I reached for the rearview mirror to get a closer look—and *bam*! It was as if someone had hurled dirt into my left eye, leaving me instantly panic-stricken. I struggled to stay in my lane, but the car swerved as I lost all sense of direction.

Then everything went pitch-black. My right eye twitched vigorously, traumatized by the instant blindness of my left. Making a hard right, I dodged hitting a tree on the side of the road and drove into a ditch. I put the car in neutral, trying to steady my hands to remove the seatbelt, and clung to the car for dear life as I felt my way around the vehicle. There had never before been a time such as this when I felt so completely removed from the physical world.

As my right eye struggled to hold on, I covered my left eye with my hand and felt my way down the road, waving my arms erratically for someone to find me. I was in desperate need of medical attention.

"Help, please!" I gestured, guided by the sounds of the wilderness.

Suddenly, Nelly B came to mind, like a dark horse in my blindness. There was a burst of obscene laughter in my ears as I heard her whisper, "I saw something coming after you, Jane." The echoes of her voice tranquilized me.

Then I heard the old woman's voice follow: "Stay away from that woman—she is treacherous!"

Overcome by hysteria, I collapsed on the side of the highway, just before I was rescued by my neighbor who was passing by. She rushed me to my optometrist, who was stunned to see me in this state of desperation.

"I don't understand. I just saw you less than a year ago, and now your test shows hemorrhaging in the back of both eyes." He took another look and added, "I'm afraid you're going to lose your left eye, possibly your right."

"No!" I screamed, grasping the doctor's arm. "There has to be something that can be done."

Somberly, he suggested a radical procedure that was rarely done back then. "We'll try a new laser therapy to see if I can repair the lens, but nothing is guaranteed."

"Nothing ever is, Doctor, but I'm willing to try."

I closed my fists tightly, as the laser came closer. I hoped that the pain would dissipate and the procedure would restore my vision. With every brushstroke of the laser penetrating deeper, I imagined Nelly's hologram etched in my blindness. The blade burned through the first layers—the smoky smell from my cornea started to nauseate my insides.

"Hold very still. Don't move an inch." The doctor's voice steadied as he went in deeper. "Almost done." His laser continued zapping away, making popping sounds like Rice Krispies in milk.

When he finished, he wrapped a heavy bandage around my eyes and phoned Tony to tell him the terrible news. It was a spellbinding horror. My thoughts played tricks on me in the darkness as I awaited his arrival. Every movement felt abnormal and disgustingly criminal as I relied on the help of others. Even the doctor's hands guiding me to the waiting room broke my spirit.

"Keep the dressing on for a few days, Jane—and on the third day, you can remove the bandages. But let me remind you, I can't guarantee the procedure will have worked."

Tony embraced me and we walked together quietly to the car. Would I ever see my children again? I was filled with dread. There was nothing anyone could do to comfort me. All I could do was wait.

Chapter 20

Uncle Thurman and
The Holy Spirit

"The Holy Spirit came to me after losing my eyesight.
Now, more than ever, the supernatural world lived inside me.
There are two sides to good and evil, and that is the sacred ground
on which we live. We could let in something unintentionally and spend
the rest of our lives trying to expel it. You can never be too careful.
Deception lingers behind the kindest face."

—JANE CORSARO

Back at home, I was at the mercy of Tony and my children to help with daily chores. I had seventy-two hours to await my fate. My senses were amplified. Even in the silence, I could feel the shadows increase, caving in on me as I rested in the stillness of the night.

For three days, I was lost in the avalanche of my misery—praying every minute to God that I could see the faces of my family again, even if for a moment. But where I was headed felt like the pits of hell—frozen, unconscious, in pain, and paranoid. Surely, Nelly would find her way into our home and murder me at my bedside without me realizing she was there. I lay in a nest of emptiness, awaiting the next hour, and the next, and the next.

When I'd hear Dean cry, I felt helpless, relying on Tony and Craig to comfort him. I was a stranger in my own body, but Nelly's cruel games were only just the beginning of my anguish. On the third day, Tony came into our bedroom to find me rocking in the recliner and solemnly quiet. The lights remained low and the curtains drawn shut.

"We'll open them just a little to start." Tony proceeded.

"But what if I can't see?" I turned my head, resisting his attempts.

He never gave up. He just came closer to rest beside me, gently patting my leg and encouraging me to trust him.

"We need to remove the bandages, just like the doctor ordered. I know you're scared, but we will navigate this," Tony whispered into my delicate ears.

His words calmed my fears as we carefully unraveled the bandages around my eyes. The circling of never-ending gauze was dizzying, as I feared the worst would greet me on the other side. Approaching the last layer, I prayed to God to see color or anything at all.

My eyelids were weak, but, as I opened my right eye, the miracle of light drew in from beyond the curtains. Tony's face was a treasure—I could see every detail of him looking back at me like the perfect gift. So, overwhelmed, I cried and fell to pieces in his embrace, sobbing like a child, saved once again like I had dodged a bullet.

After a few days, the vision in my right eye returned, but it never fully recovered. However, my left eye was left permanently blind. I would wear a prosthesis for two years before receiving my permanent implant, which would lead me down a course of uncomfortable injections every month to retain my right eye. My diagnosis reported a hemorrhaging disorder that only happens in rare circumstances. None of the specialists I saw had any answers.

But I did.

In the two years that would follow, my entire routine was mapped out. I could no longer drive, so I walked my boys to the bus stop instead. The city transit became a lifesaver, allowing me to still take care of my household and Mum's, just as I had before. Willfully, I embraced my disability as a strength rather than a weakness and once more weathered the storms in front of me.

"I know who did this to you, Mum," Craig confessed one evening while helping set the dinner table. "It was Nelly. I'm sure of it. Ever since you went blind, she hasn't come around anymore. Haven't you noticed?"

At once, I changed the conversation, although I knew deep down that Craig's intuition was right, as it always was.

"Let's not discuss her right now. I think we've all had enough of her presence. Anyhow, how are you and Andrea?" I asked, pouring the milk.

"We broke up again." Craig opened the newspaper to act distracted.

"Broke up? Oh, sweetie, I'm sorry. What happened?"

"Nothing. She just wants some time apart," Craig said, excusing himself to wash up.

Andrea danced around Craig's heart like a merry-go-round, breaking up with him to date other people and then getting back together with him when she became homesick for his affections. My son's devotion to her ran deeper than time itself, even at such an early age. He was consumed by her power and lost himself in her heart.

Later that evening, I could hear Craig on the phone. I softly nudged open the door to listen.

"Andrea, you know I love you!" he shouted. "What more do you want from me?"

Although I felt compelled to come between them, there is a time in a mother's life when all she can do is listen. Even if the pain claws at you, your child's heart must remain free.

"What is it, Mommy?" Dean tugged at my nightgown.

"Nothing, honey. Let's get you back to your room." I scooted him off to bed in a hurry.

The next morning, I tore out the weeds along the front yard, distracted by my son's conversation. One by one, I yanked the stubborn roots from their beds, trying to separate my emotions from his growing pains.

Cora had been calling me nonstop, begging me to pick up cigarettes. It was her way of drowning out her loneliness. Her doctors argued with her time and time again to quit, but Mum continued to smoke three packs a day, inhaling them like they were sugar sticks, perhaps to fight off her own demons and ease her depression. She was battling a degenerative bone disease that required third-degree wound care. Mum was tougher than nails, but if it hadn't been for the codeine tablets, she would have died sooner.

"It's about damn time you answered!" she snipped. "When can you come by to pick up my grocery list?"

Unnerved by her demands, I tried not to raise my voice. "It will be a few hours, Mum. I have some things to finish here at the house."

"Well, alright, but I'm almost dead, Jane. You realize my cigs are the only thing I've got left," she scoffed, trying to make me feel guilty.

She was at it again, trying to provoke me with her cutting sarcasm as I worked hard to calm my anger. Then another call interrupted us.

"I just told you I would be there in a few hours!" I yelled, losing my patience.

"Well, hello, Jane. It's Nelly. Sounds like you're having a rough day. Listen, do you think Tony and you could help me out? I didn't make enough rent money to pay the power bill this month, and without heat, Leonard and I will freeze over the winter. I'll pay you back—I promise."

Nelly B had repeatedly come to Tony and me for favors over the years. We'd always give in just to keep her content. Honestly, I feared her reckless mind and the incubus that controlled it. Paying her off and keeping her contained made me feel like I was easing her sickness, at least temporarily.

"Just this one time, Nelly," I said, ending the conversation before she could say more.

Her voice sounded heavy, like a fire-breathing dragon. "Thank you, Jane."

Cora and Nelly were like splints in my spine, holding me straight enough to fend them off, but slumped when they left me high and dry. They had access to my injuries. If I'd have gone insane, Nelly would have been on my porch steps with handcuffs, and Cora would have signed off on the papers.

As the years continued onward, my mind was like a freight train working overtime to stay ahead of Nelly. Our home was turned upside down with secrets left unresolved until the next callous spell would come rapping at our door.

That's when I turned to the Holy Spirit to seek answers, leading me to my Uncle Thurman, who ran a church at the center of town.

I'd met him only a handful of times when I was younger. Cora thought fondly of him and praised him for his fellowship with the Lord, but they co-existed in opposite worlds. And despite the apprehension I had toward pastors, Uncle Thurman wasn't a pedophile, nor did he run a cult. That made me feel safe entering a world that was foreign and raw to me. I had always wanted to belong.

Uncle Thurman was married to his faith and richer in values than even Cora had realized. Ever since he was a child, he'd been glued to the Bible. He could see and feel the trinity at his fingertips and prophesized things that no one else could explain, setting him apart from just any ordinary theologian.

• • •

A Cold Winters Night - 1984

Tony and Dean stayed back while Craig and I rode the first bus into town. The ride over potholes made for a bumpy journey, but I was more concerned by Craig's silence. It had been weeks since he spoke to Andrea.

"Are you all right, Craig?" I asked.

"I'm fine. I just have a lot on my mind right now," he said, staring out the window, seemingly removed from his surroundings.

"I'm looking forward to this evening. It will be good for the both of us." I watched his breathing quicken as he focused his eyes on the passing streetlights and ignored my presence.

There wasn't any magic I could conjure up to mend his broken spirit. My heart pounded with prejudice against Andrea's spell on my boy, but I understood this "love story" all too well. John immediately entered my mind, but I dismissed the passionate replay and skipped over it like a rock skimming the water.

When the bus's brakes squealed to a halt, Craig and I made our way up the church steps. I held securely to his coat. The faint images and church lights looked like angelic figurines dipped in gold. Warmed by the beautiful foyer of cathedral chandeliers, we made our way into the main hall and found our seats. I set my purse beside me and planted my eyes on the enormous wooden cross where it was lifted for all to see. Overcome by the candlelight's flames that enriched my spirit on the mantles, I contained myself from weeping. The smell of roses was heavenly, and the harmonic timbre of the pipe organ tugged at my heartstrings as if to welcome us home.

"I love you," I said, resting my head on Craig's shoulder.

"Love you too, Mum," he said, studying the interior framework in admiration.

After a few minutes, Uncle Thurman entered with conviction and spoke. His message was rich with scripture, right from the wisdom of God himself. Suddenly my heart felt harvested and not shut out. Uncle

Thurman could resurrect the child in me and the tiny soul that hid within.

"There is a young man who is with us tonight. A young man who better come to the altar and give himself to God, or he'll never get another chance." He patiently looked over the crowd.

Craig struggled to pay attention after noticing a young lady across the pew staring at him. Taken by her gesture, their eyes entertained their intentions, although Craig remained modest in silence. I grabbed his hand to summon his attention back to the sermon.

"There is a young man this evening who needs to ask God for forgiveness," he repeated, sweeping the floor with corrective eyes while the young and old remained silent.

I wanted to distract Craig from the lady of mystery, but I didn't want to disturb others, especially in a house of worship. However, Uncle Thurman's sermon would haunt me forever—I would always wonder if I should have begged Craig to head to the altar that evening. I couldn't have known the importance, unless I was God himself, because I was broken like the rest of them.

Distracted by Craig and the young girl's rendezvous, I couldn't help but notice her youthful beauty. From what I could distinguish with my poor eyesight, she had a natural magnetism about her and a heart-shaped face with blonde wavy tresses.

Uncle Thurman bowed his head. "Let us pray."

After the service ended, Craig quickly went over to meet the pretty blonde and offered his number before she disappeared into the crowd.

I watched in awe, noticing his countenance boost with confidence. Then I took in one last glance at the altar before saying good night to Uncle Thurman, who embraced me for the first time in years.

"Take good care of Craig. He seems like a fine young man." He smiled across the room toward my son. "God be with him."

"Thank you, pastor. I'll let him know."

We arrived back home that evening to be greeted by Tony and Dean playing board games in the front parlor.

"Well, someone looks happy to have gone to church," Tony said, noticing Craig's disposition.

"Don't ask." I shooed Tony to the bedroom. "He met a girl this evening," I said under my breath.

Tony seemed impressed as he followed me with his bag of popcorn.

That night, before retiring to bed, I said a prayer:

Dear Heavenly Father, I pray for my son Craig.
Please watch over him and protect him from his heartache.
I pray for your strength and guidance, dear Lord,
as you continue to lead and heal our family. Amen.

My son might not have gone to the altar that night, but I went for him—the Holy Spirit surely knew that. Craig was fragile but strong, just as God intended him to be. There was nothing I could do or say as he grew older and formed his own independence, away from my protection. I feared the fire that burned inside him. It was just like mine, but it was innocently deceived.

Uncle Thurman's message was truth. When we try to uphold the world, we all fall down. I tried to become the hero for my family, but I couldn't rescue them all, not even with God by my side. Sometimes, we aren't built for taming storms. Sometimes, we're just built for enduring the aftermath.

Although my vision had failed me, my sixth sense was becoming stronger. Something was coming back for us.

• • •

"It haunted me over my entire life as to why I had to endure
so much hardship, but even with all I have to express,
I will still die someday without saying it all. We are imperfect.
We have all sinned. We cannot begin to understand the greatness of
our Creator because we cannot even begin to explain our own existence.
Our words get mixed up while trying to solve equations
from stars, but they only get lost in infinity.

Man comes up empty-handed. He becomes arguably wicked
in his ways to maintain power because he has none.
It's as simple as that. We hold on to nothing by our grasp, yet
humankind will fight to rule countries, kill, hoard, corrupt, deceive,
and ignore the simplest truth: Our last chapter is death.

Your entire life will end up with one final moment,
one last breath, and a memory. I awoke to this truth
early on when God found me alone in the wild.
Trust his plan and not your own."

—JANE CORSARO

Chapter 21

MESSAGE FROM ABOVE

*"I've walked the darkest streets and run from wolves, but I always
returned stronger. Since I was a child, walking had become a normal
survival skill to calm my fear of the unknown. When I was hurt,
in pain, and had nothing to lean on, I'd walk. Not out of shame but out
of pride. Even when I couldn't see, I'd learned my way around the world,
playing Monopoly with the American Dream and empowering my mind
to believe I'd already won the game. Although my sight had diminished,
my intuition intensified, and I'd grown closer to God. He gave me
the strength to channel all my fears and doubts like a cluster of
pigeon seed I poured into nature. I repented with each step."*

—JANE CORSARO

April 1984

Seemingly overnight, Dean was approaching seven. The older he
became, the more he'd soak up Craig's mannerisms. On clear nights,
I'd watch the two of them stargaze. Dean would eagerly point to shooting stars and listen to Craig share stories about space, pretending they

were captains on a mission. The two of them would sit on the porch for hours, staring up at the inky blackness with eager eyes.

"Do you see that? Look! It's right up there." Craig pointed to the North Star. "One day, I'm going to explore space."

"I want to go too!" Dean insisted. "Wherever you go, I've got to go with you." He smiled up at Craig.

"Alright, little man, but right now, I think it's past your bedtime. We'll talk more about my space travels another night." Craig piggy-backed Dean to bed.

As the moon's reflection settled onto my aging face, I heard the porch door open, and Melonie, Craig's new girlfriend from church, and he greeted each other. Rinsing the soapsuds off the remaining dishes, I watched as they made their way toward the park.

It had been almost a year since Andrea had broken up with my son, but it was hard to tell where his heart was. Even under the street-lights, I could see—or sense—the tug of war. Melonie yearned for him, but he was consumed by something else. She wasn't outspoken like Andrea, who challenged Craig's clever mind. Melonie was a modest girl, sweet and harmonious, gentle and soft-spoken. She adored Craig. You could see it in her eyes and feel it, but I knew it wasn't enough to satisfy his hunger.

As they walked away and their laughter faded, a vortex within my soul took me back in time to my mother's house.

Cora had peered out her windowpane, tracing the lengthy vines with her tired eyes. There were cadaverous spider vines that crept and crawled up the siding of her home, day after day, week after week, and year after year, until they swallowed the house whole, leaving her buried alive.

Then suddenly, in my mind, I was standing next to Chuck's death-bed. He and Cora had been sick for years. And although he'd tried to make amends during family gatherings, my forgiveness was dormant. Chuck's malevolence mutated in his body like a secondary sickness, and there wasn't a cure for it. The county nursing home smelled of rotting feces, uninhabitable for any human. I stared down into his pitted eyes and malnourished skin and bones—there was an odd sorrow. I remember him taking shallow breaths as I sat at his bedside, waiting impatiently for him to die.

I never told him I loved him because a goodbye seemed enough. Chuck's daughter squeezed his hand, unaware of our past, then his eyes rotated to look out the window as he gasped for air. Cruel as it may seem, he had built the walls of his prison, and the sparse light from the outside corridors was a reminder of the light he avoided in life.

His dilated eyes finally landed on me—his puppet. He gripped my hand with force like he was screaming for mercy, but I couldn't forget the beatings or the way he made me feel unwanted as a child. The images of my piggybank smashed into my heart. Thelma's scars and bruises returned, and the vengeance he laid upon me as a child wept in my soul. My humanity was raw as I choked back tears, seeing him struggle in his hospital bed because he could no longer hurt me!

"I was just a child!" my voice screamed from within. But quiet in hurt, I was drowning inside, watching his lungs obstruct and sound the death rattle. When that hour struck, distress overcame me, because even death wasn't enough. It just wiped away a perpetrator, but it left the horrors behind.

Slap, boom, bang! The wrath of his fists could be felt across my body as I felt his own body dying before me. Slap, boom, bang! I could taste the blood pooling in my mouth and leaving its dirty mark. Slap, boom, bang! I saw my battered face staring back at me in the mirror. Slap, boom, bang! I saw his heartless eyes on the playground watching me cry out for help as he did nothing! Slap, boom, bang! It was all over. I opened my eyes and saw him frozen. His daughter wailed out in agony, and, in a matter of minutes, our story had ended. She knew him as her daddy, and I knew him as my enemy.

• • •

"You, OK?" Tony asked, startling me from my daydream.

"Yeah, I was just thinking." I turned away to wipe my eyes.

"Thinking? Of what? How beautiful you are?" Tony sweetly pursued me, placing his arms around my waist.

"I love you, Tony. Do you know how much I love you?" His tenderness captivated me.

"I love you too." He winked.

My husband could always make me forget my fears. He charmed me with his surprises and was the devoted family man I always knew he would be—and he loved us more than I'd ever realized and deeper than I'd ever known. And despite Nelly B and all that made it complicated, our love endured through every season and every hardship.

• • •

The spring rains had washed away our sorrows, uncovering a fresh scent of rose bushes lining each neighbor's yard. The honeybees celebrated, and the bluebirds corralled together in synchronized voyages across the rooftops of our town. Spring was finally here.

"Look at the rainbow in the sky. Isn't it beautiful?" I showed Dean as I strolled to the bus stop under our umbrella. We'd left just after the heavy rain and took our time to admire the small things that caught our attention, whether it was rainbows in the sky or the butterflies leaving their floral tar mats. The natural world around us was in full bloom.

Walking toward the yellow school bus was one of my favorite parts of motherhood. I'd wave excitedly, watching Dean's adorable face press against the window glass to blow me a kiss goodbye.

That day in McKeesport had been one of the most beautiful days I'd ever seen. Collapsing my umbrella so I could feel the warm drizzle of rain touch my skin, I twirled around in circles, immersed in its serenity. But just then, something I had never experienced before occurred. A voice entered my mind like an undeniable marker—a voice that rattled me and unearthed every trepidation in my soul.

"Someone will not be walking to this bus stop next year."

Immediately, I unraveled, looking for a human person to curse. But I was alone. The message was ominous. As clear as you hear the living, I was hearing the supernatural. Panicked, I quickly rushed to Mum's, trying to keep my mind from losing control.

"Mum! Mum, where are you?" I made my way inside to find her wheelchair parked by her knitting table.

She seemed melancholy, slowly sipping her coffee, distracted by the birds.

"I know this is going to sound crazy, but this morning, after dropping Dean off at the bus stop, I received this cryptic message in the park."

Her eyes looked blank as she tried to comprehend my hysteria.

"This voice told me that someone would not be coming to that bus stop next year. I heard it as clear as I am speaking to you—you've got to believe me!" I knelt at her side. "I think it means I'm going to die. It had to be some kind of premonition. I'm sure of it!"

She gently touched my forehead. "Jane, do you really believe the voices in your head?"

"It wasn't in my mind. It was as if somebody else were standing right next to me, warning me of something terrible," I persisted. "Why would I make something like this up?" I continued to argue, rethinking every moment since breakfast.

"Well, if it wasn't you, who was it then, Jane?" She stirred her coffee and stared into my eyes with motherly concern.

"Mum, something is trying to protect me. It felt like a message from a divine entity, a message from above. Call it what you want, but something is trying to prepare me." Suddenly, my voice grew silent. "And if it means I'm going to die, what will happen to my children?"

Her face turned pale at the thought. "I'm not sure I have the answer, Jane."

That afternoon, she and I saw God in the same light—we just didn't know his plan.

There are always powerful messages that come and go in our lives. Sometimes these messages are transmitted into different frequencies that shouldn't be ignored, even when they feel irrational for going against logic. It's the spiritual world that delivers us.

"Jane, keep ahold of yourself—but in the meantime, keep watch on your surroundings." She became uncomfortably silent. Cora wasn't one to believe in coincidences such as this, but somehow, I knew she believed me, although it was too frightening to consider the truth.

• • •

After I returned home, the message I received that day left me feeling isolated. To this very day, whenever I speak of it, I feel alone. I had no one to turn to. It was like I was planning my funeral in silence, without the comfort of family or a final resting place for a headstone.

Of course, I didn't want to alarm my family. If the premonition was correct, maybe it would be a swift death, and I'd expire in my sleep. Maybe the wolves would snatch me by the river, or maybe I would just vanish into thin air. There wasn't a logical way to think about it. And although Nelly B came into the back of my mind, confronting her on the matter was out of the question. That would just land me in the psychiatric hospital.

I thought it would all blow over, until I received an unexpected phone call.

"Hello?" Nelly's son struggled to speak. "It's ... I'm calling ... because my mother ... is speaking to them ... again."

"I don't understand. What are you trying to tell me, Leonard? Who is *them*? What is she talking to?" My voice began to shake.

"Shadow people. She's been ... been speaking to ... them."

"How do you know this?" I said, trying hard to keep his attention on track.

"Mother says she doesn't like y-y-you. She wants you to stay ... to stay away, and she asked bad people how ... how she can fix things." His voice trailed off after that.

Desperate, I whispered into the phone so Tony couldn't hear my plea. "I need you to tell me exactly what you heard and saw."

"I ... I have to go. Mother is coming."

I struggled to hear through the static. But then the line cut out.

I immediately went to the back room and said a prayer for my family. Within the weeks that followed, I asked Tony to add locks to all our windows. He didn't argue, and he never asked me why. Maybe he already knew that Nelly couldn't be trusted.

• • •

As Christmas Eve approached, I was brought back to the warning I'd received at the bus stop, but I ignored it and rolled up my sleeves to glaze the turkey, hoping it was all just a figment of my imagination.

Our Christmas tree was perfect, and we all gathered around to sing carols. Melonie hung the last of the ornaments as I caught Dean sneaking all the candy canes into his pajama pockets.

After scooting Dean off to change for bedtime, I had a moment to reconnect with Craig who was watching Melonie from afar.

"Do you love her?" I placed my arm around him.

Craig looked pleasantly surprised I had asked the question. "Yes, of course."

"Well, have you given it any thought yet?" I smiled, adoring Melonie's sweet glances over at us.

"If you're talking about marriage, of course, I've thought about it. But right now, we're taking things one step at a time." He smiled back at her, and I at him.

After the festivities had ended, in the wee hours of the night, I dreamed of the message in the park once more.

As I basked in the sunshine, golden rays poured from rich barrels, like a drape over my body. There were no clouds or earthly portraits, only vast configurations of lights for millions of miles. But all too soon, the rising hoofs of hades stampeded through my soul like a twelve-gauge shotgun.

"Someone will not be coming to the bus stop next year!"

Suddenly, I awoke in a cold sweat, struggling for air. I ran to put on my bathrobe and check on Craig and Dean, who were sound asleep, undisturbed by my presence. I tiptoed to the front door, opened it, and nearly froze as the wind stole my breath away. I held tight to the doorknob as the air cut me in half. But the only thing I could feel was my heart being driven away.

"What are you trying to tell me!?" I shouted to the angels of the night, but the wind remained strong, like a masquerade of white ghosts digging my grave in the snow.

"God give me strength."

Chapter 22

A KING IN TURMOIL

The child in me clawed at my insides to escape. It was too much to handle, not knowing what life had in store for us all. By masking my fears, I appeared to have it all under control.

Even the actress inside me was taxed from the roles I'd had to reprise time and time again. I didn't want to go on performing for Nelly B or anyone else for that matter. After crying out to the wind, I lived out each day as if it were my last. My family, especially my boys, was the light that kept me going.

"I've got some great news, Mum. I'm going to propose to Melonie this weekend." Craig caught me by surprise as he loosened his tie.

"That's wonderful, sweetheart!"

"I already have the perfect spot, and I've been saving up for the ring—I hope she'll like it." He revealed the tiny diamond in his palm.

"I'm sure she'll love it. She's a lucky girl."

But his face seemed too composed and compiled with questions.

"Mum, how do you know for sure?" He looked at me with his large green eyes.

"Well, honey … It's just a feeling. You'll know when it's the right time," I said, returning to sit down.

Craig had been dating Melonie for over a year, but somehow, I knew Andrea always had my son's heart. The wool couldn't be pulled over my eyes. I could see right through the orchestration Craig was conducting. It could have fooled anyone, but not me. Not his mother. Behind the surface, his emotions for Andrea were locked away. Like a king in turmoil, he yearned for his queen.

Craig had a sensitive heart and explored his feelings through poetry. He'd read it quietly to himself, repeating his favorite verses aloud. His affection for Melonie was different from the romantic feelings he'd had for Andrea, and I knew it was only time until the castle walls around his heart would break.

A few weeks past New Year's, I realized that he hadn't proposed, so I approached him, concerned by his cold demeanor and deteriorating stature.

"How is everything with Melonie?" I asked.

"We're fine." He shoved some papers into his desk, pushing them to the back. "Why do you always have to barge in? Can't you knock? "He stormed past me, frustrated by my presence.

"What's the matter with you, Craig? I was only asking a question. We haven't seen Melonie over here in some time, and—"

"We're taking a break. I don't feel like discussing everything with you and the entire family. You stick to your life and let me live mine!" Craig fired, looking through me instead of at me.

But instead of letting him walk away, I followed him to the kitchen.

"Don't raise your voice in this house. I'm just concerned, that's all. You stay in your room for hours, you're barely present at the dinner table—"

"Well, don't be concerned!" He snapped, slamming the fridge door and returning to his bedroom.

His outbursts made me sick with worry, and I'll admit, I was scared he was allowing Andrea to rule his affections. But he appeared to have decided she was the one, refusing any intervention from Tony and me. So, I had no choice but to watch my son seclude himself in his own fantasies beyond my reach. He drifted further from our lives and into a world I never knew.

. . .

January 1985

"Will you just speak to me? Damn it! What's the matter with you?" I banged on Craig's door one evening while Dean was home, sick with the flu. That night, Tony had stayed late after work.

Craig threw open his bedroom door, looking like a frail corpse driven with insanity. "The matter with me? What the hell's the matter with you? Never mind. I'm getting out of here!" He flung open the closet, grabbing his things and stuffing them into a suitcase.

"You won't even talk to us anymore. Why can't you just let Andrea go, Craig? She's gone. Let her go!" I blocked him in the hallway, desperate for him to reconsider, but he pushed past me, driven by his own demons.

"What is it about Andrea that bothers you? You don't know the kind of relationship we had. All you do is judge her!"

Craig idled as I tried to stop him from leaving. "What does it matter if I still love her? What would that mean to you anyways?"

His empty stare concerned me. Then the telephone rang, leaving us a moment to surrender.

"If it's Melonie calling, tell her I'm not here!" Craig yelled as he turned to pack the last of his things.

"Hello?"

"Hello, Mrs. Corsaro. It's Andrea. May I please speak to Craig? I really need to talk to him—it's important."

"Andrea, you need to stop this with my son! You've played enough with his heart; I won't let you hurt him again! Weren't you aware that he's engaged to somebody else?" I impinged on her, only to regret overstepping my boundaries.

I'll never forget Andrea's abrupt silence at that moment. It will haunt me forever. There was just a faint cry, and then the phone died.

"Who was that?" Craig marched past me, stopping just before he kicked open the door.

"Andrea," I said, faintly.

"Andrea? What did you say to her?" He rushed over, shaking me by the shoulders to demand answers.

But I wouldn't budge. Instead, I held onto the phone, desperately trying to keep him from grabbing it, although I wish I would have let it go.

I confessed and broke into tears.

"I told her you proposed to someone else… I'm so sorry, Craig. I crossed the line, but I did it to save you. You need to let her go!"

His eyes deposited a sharp syringe into my heart as he towered over me.

"Save me? Save me from what? Myself? You had no business intervening like that." His voice became dangerously calm.

"I'm so sorry, Craig."

There was nothing I could have done to console him, he made it clear after he pushed my hands away and disappeared into the basement, a place he often went to build his models. Guilt-stricken by my actions, I bowed my head to ask the Lord for forgiveness. But as I confessed my sin, I was interrupted by a loud, invasive banging that couldn't be ignored.

I wiped my eyes and took notice of the uneasy silence within the house. Immediately, I called out for Craig. But there was no answer as I stared at the basement door.

When I turned the knob, the little vision I had left led me down the concrete steps. In front of me, there was only a sparse glow from the moonlight filtering through the window. To my presumption, I had thought the dryer was plugged from an overflow of clothing, so I went to repair it. But to my horror, I stumbled into Craig's legs, hanging from the rafters.

As I felt the soles of his shoes mid-air, I lost my breath. Panic-stricken, I pulled the light switch on and saw his body hoovering above me, next to the dryer. My mind detached from reality as my entire world came crashing down. Unable to recognize the shock, I thought Craig had been levitated by some evil force, but what had actually happened was a suicide. The sight drove a stake into my heart. My ability to breathe and to scream was obliterated. In that desperate moment of hell, I begged for God's mercy while harnessing every instinct in my body to save him!

Next to Tony's toolbox I spotted a knife and cut him from the rope, frantically sawing the blade back and forth to free him from strangulation. On the last cut, his lifeless body fell into my embrace, pinning me to the floor as I screamed a mother's ungodly cry. Craig was dead. My son was dead! In the darkest trench I'd ever known, I held him in my arms. He was wearing the clothes he wore for Christmas. I could smell the cologne on his skin as I rolled him onto his back trying to breathe life into his lungs. But when no signs of life appeared, I screamed into his sweater like a soldier at war. My trembling hands delicately touched the black and blue marks around his neckline from lack of oxygen.

"Mommy, Mommy!" Dean cried out from the top of the stairs. "Are you OK?"

Suddenly, my protective instincts kicked in. "Mommy will be up soon—go to your room!"

I held Craig like a baby in my arms, weeping uncontrollably, and noticed the milk which he drank earlier that evening pour from the sides of his lips.

The only wish I had for God was for him to take me, but he wouldn't allow it! I could have hung myself because I felt I deserved it. Why did God save me?!

Tony was coming through the door when I hollered for an ambulance, but there was no pulse.

My little Craig's life flashed before my eyes. In my mind, his handsome smile looked back at me as he danced around like a child.

"Remember, Craigy, what I told you when Alfie died? Beyond the sunset is love with God in heaven. All things go beyond the sunset ... past the moon and stars, way far away from here. It's a place you can't touch but that always lives inside your heart. Now make your way far beyond the sunset to heaven."

I sobbed over his lifeless body.

"Mommy loves you, baby. Mommy loves you." I cradled him in my arms, rocking him until the ambulance arrived. They pronounced my boy dead at the scene. I turned violent as they tried to retrieve his body. I shoved them away, but they eased my grasp from his sweater, and I passed away in spirit at that moment.

"Don't let them take my boy!" I reached for Craig's body, then turned to pound at Tony's chest as he held me securely. I fell to the cement ground, clawing at the grooves until my nails bled.

Nothing in my life was more excruciating than that moment. Nothing ever will be. How could I tell Dean his brother wasn't coming back? Tony couldn't contain himself as he watched the body being taken away. Craig's death broke us all.

For weeks, I could neither eat nor sleep. My depression had every-one concerned, but I resisted medication. It might have been easier to numb the pain, but I had to feel it. I had to feel every bit for Craig's sake. I was lost with no answers, while I searched his room for clues. Until I stumbled upon a poem he had recently written for Andrea. There are no words to express how I felt reading it.

Well, I have lost you fairly.

In my own way and with my full consent.

Say what you will, but rarely, no king in turmoil
went to his death, prouder than this one went.

Some nights of apprehension and hot weeping I will confess,
days dried my eyes for that's permitted me.

Rubbed in a rage. A wing that would be set free.

Should I love you less, or played you slyly, I might have
held you for a summer more.

But at the cost of words, I value highly no such summer
as the one before.

Should I outlive the anguish as all men do?

I should have only good to say of you, I'd still die for you.

Love, Craig

His tears had stained the paper and his eyeglasses. I hid the poem right then and there because I couldn't live to be reminded. I felt guilt for not discovering my son's pain sooner.

• • •

When I buried my Craig, I disappeared. I vanished into the background. Neighbors would ask me how I found the courage to cut his rope, like I were a goddamn hero.

They said they were sorry, but I couldn't understand what that meant. Craig wasn't coming back. Sorry, to me, meant the possibility of reconciliation or that it was possible to forgive and forget. Sorry meant that they could feel my pain, when they couldn't—or sorry meant I don't know what to say, but sorry sounds better in a crisis. It's honest because there are truly no words anyone can offer.

The rain poured, causing the mud to form swamps across the cemetery grounds. We held our umbrellas high above our heads, but I would have rather sunk into the earth. I knew I had to carry on for Dean and Tony. But unless you've lost a child, you won't understand how hard it is to explain the difficulty in getting up each day and going to bed each night.

I remember his high school teacher offered his condolences after the ceremony.

"I'm so sorry, Jane. Craig was a magnificent man. I'm disturbed by this news and don't know what to say. He had such a bright future."

I didn't respond, but Tony thanked him as we moved through the crowd of heavy faces.

There were so many people there to pay their respects, but Mum's anguish capsized me. I could barely look at her. It was disbelief. It was a shock. She and I had shared so much in this life, but she could never know my pain, not even in her own hell.

I made my way toward Melonie at the end of the line. She was crying in her mother's arms. We couldn't look at each other, not then. There was a thorn in my heart as I left everyone on the hill where Craig's body was laid to rest.

Back at home, the rains cleared as evening set upon us. God must have been mourning with me because I noticed a beautiful sunset forming over our favorite hillside. Tears poured in my silent suffering.

My baby boy had made it home. It was a journey of his, far from this place and higher than the rolling hillsides, where Alfie and the moon and stars would shine forever. Someday, but not today, I would join him beyond the sunset.

• • •

"I wanted to offer my condolences," Nelly said.

Her tone rankled me. But I was ready for her. She was cruel and indecent, to say the least, as she offered her sympathies.

"I was talking to my neighbor Doris and telling her about you. She said how dearly you paid in this life, losing your eyesight and your son." She rambled along as I felt my insides cave. I knew it wasn't her neighbor who said that because her neighbor didn't know me. It was Nelly's insanity speaking again.

Whether she had a conspiracy against my family or whether she wanted my blood, she already had it. I had given her everything: access to my life, my home, and my family.

I should have taken my son's place. I was so sure that what I had heard at that bus stop was for me. It was my premonition—not my son's.

Craig was only nineteen when he committed suicide, and what I've learned is that even kings have turmoil. Strong men like him who possess strength in society hide too. We all have secrets. If we didn't, we wouldn't pretend that everything is all right when it's not.

I'll never just assume people are fine anymore because we never truly get to know what's under the surface. Until we work from within, the healing can never fully start.

Chapter 23

LIFE AFTER DEATH

Since Craig's passing, I have spent my life trying to solve the mystery of Uncle Thurman's sermon, the premonition near the bus stop, and Nelly's curse on my family. I truly believe to this very day that it was, indeed, a curse. But the mystery is still unsolved.

Our family tried to get along, but we fell to pieces in our grief. One day, Dean cried in the back seat as we took him to school.

"I want my brother back! He promised he'd always be here. How could he break his promise?" Dean pushed his palms into his eyes, which were already red and swollen from exhaustion.

I couldn't find the words to ease his pain, but a few minutes later, Tony did.

"I'm going to be here for you," Tony said over his shoulder. "Everything Craig promised, I'm going to do for you." He stretched his hand back for Dean to grab. And just like that, Dean was reassured by his father's compassion. He reached out, tightly squeezing his father's hand.

Tony became Dean's hero. From that moment on, they would do everything together, just as Tony promised.

There is life after death. Maybe not the same as you would imagine it. For us and for the sake of our son, it meant moving forward, one day at a time. God had shed his mercy on us, and I was certain that he exists—otherwise, I wouldn't be here to tell my story, and you wouldn't be here to read it. I believed then as I do now: We all have a story, a purpose, a place, and a time.

Back then, for me, there were still some things about Craig's death that had me searching for answers. To reclaim my sanity, I continued to research, which led me to a well-known psychic who lived just beyond the edge of town. Past the gullies of a forest and hidden from everyday travelers, her place was a well-kept secret from aristocrats who searched for adventure but were too conservative to believe in the supernatural.

Tony and I pulled up the muddy road and parked to one side. He waited in the car as I walked in past the piles of dusty bookshelves and the slow-burning incense that released an aromatic plume of smoke around my body. Bottles of earthy concoctions and crucifixes lined the walls.

But it was her presence that caught me by surprise.

"I know why you're here," the wise woman hinted in a rich accent as she appeared in front of the velvet drapes. "You're here to get away from her, aren't you? Come closer, have a seat." She grabbed my hands and placed them on the table, studying them like a science experiment.

"Dear God—you have witchcraft around you." She turned to grab a deck of cards, placing them out strategically in front of me.

"Look … here!" She pressed her finger on one of the cards. "There's a woman. She's come into your life and, undoubtedly, is evil. Make no mistake, she wants to break you and your family—she'll stop at nothing to get what she wants."

She continued to study each symbol, then added, "You've paid the price for letting her in. Her cruel magic gets stronger by the day, but it appears to have followed you, even when she's not around."

Her concentration began to take on a hypnotic resonance.

"It's hard for me to see past the cards, but this woman has conjured up Satan himself. Take this with you!" Her concern appeared deeper as she handed me a crucifix and wrapped rosary beads around my hands to pray.

"Whatever you do, don't let her back into your life. She'll try everything, but unless you resist her temptations, she will continue to take away everything you love."

I looked up from clenching the rosary in my fists, gripped by fear. "What about my family?" I said under my breath.

Her wild eyes said it all when she bid her final piece of advice: "You have a powerful mind—you'll know what to do. Just remember the light; it's a gift. When you learn how to use it, nothing can harm you."

Thanking her profusely, I slid the rosary into my pocket as I hurried toward the car. I never told Tony what she'd said. It was something I had to resolve on my own because, after all, Nelly B wanted me next.

• • •

Later that week, from my kitchen window, I saw Nelly coming up the pathway. She was admiring my rose garden. From afar, she appeared pleasant, like an ordinary woman, but her knock at my door was anything but friendly.

"I was in the area and wanted to bring you these," she said, offering me a bouquet of wildflowers.

"No, thank you. I have plenty from the funeral," I responded coldly, refusing to take them.

"Oh." She paused. "I see. Well, I was just at the church and bottled up some holy water. I know how stressful life has been for you lately. Perhaps this would offer some comfort."

"No, thank you. I have everything I need right here."

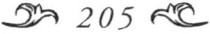

Nelly's eyes strained as I went to shut the screen door.

"Surely, you'll need some help. After all, your eyesight is gone, and someone will have to drive you around town from time to time." She clearly was juggling around to find a reason to stay.

"I've already walked this town blindly, Nelly. You know that."

"Oh, alright then!" Her failed bargaining upset her. "Considering the terrible things that have happened to you, it's just a shame you won't let me into your life, even after all the things I've done for you and your family."

But Nelly's tantrum didn't intimidate me. Instead, I confronted the woman who despised just the thought of my existence, a person whose codependency on our lives was her obsession and whose callous ways were a game. I was standing before a monster in disguise, deceitful and full of revenge.

In those last moments, I knew that Nelly had no power over me. She was just a miserable woman whom I had allowed into our lives without knowing the consequences—but this time I was ready for her.

"I don't want you over here anymore, Nelly. In fact, I don't want you anywhere near my property. My family is not yours!"

Nelly's eyes spawned the demon I always knew was there. And just like that, I could see it being sucked down inside her. Her face drained, expressionless. It was the quickest I'd ever seen her depart.

That afternoon, I swept her wickedness from my front porch like sawdust, and I stood in my glory, feeling the chains around my ankles finally release.

"Who was that?" Tony shouted.

"Nobody. It was just another salesperson trying to offer unwanted goods." I stared out the door, shutting the screen behind me.

Later that evening, I went to check on Dean. "Whatcha working on?" I whispered.

"Just some homework from school." He set his pencil aside while hiding behind his textbook.

"I think it would be good if we all got away for a while, don't you think? How about we go to the lake? We'll take our camping gear and shut out the noise for a while."

His eyes peeked over, relieved to escape his studies.

Tony and I loaded the camper the next day and hit the open road. At camp, we could see the stars shine brilliantly above. Up here, the stars twinkled like sparkling diamonds, igniting our hearts with wonder. It had been Craig's favorite place.

As we huddled around the fire, the embers sparked and crackled, leaving our eyes mesmerized by the flames.

"Do you think he's up there?" Dean pointed to the North Star.

"Of course, I do. If anyone could've got there, it would have been your brother. He knew the stars better than anyone."

But my attempt to honor Craig's memory angered Dean. "He promised me he'd always be here. He promised, but he left me behind!" He threw a stick into the mud and stood up to brush himself off. "I don't understand!" he said, pacing back and forth. "Why didn't he love us enough to stay?"

Although I would have done anything to take the pain away, I had to watch it erode the laughter in his heart. But Tony remained his hero. His father meant everything to him, and I couldn't blame him for that. He needed a man who could hold things together. And that's what Tony did when life felt like it was coming apart. He tried to save us all.

Chapter 24

UNINVITED

*"I couldn't have gotten away from Nelly, even if I'd tried.
The moment I married Tony, I inherited her
like a birthmark on my skin."*

—JANE CORSARO

Mum and I continued to go to the hillsides as long as she was able. I'd push her creaking wheelchair with all my might up the grassy lawns where we'd sit to admire our last sunsets together. It was a place of healing, a land of remorse and solitude. It offered forgiveness and new life passageways.

"What do you remember about when I was young?" I asked, watching her sit contently while soaking in the sunshine.

"I remember our life wasn't easy. I'd made some poor decisions, but I tried my best to erase the things I couldn't make up for, Jane." She picked at the petals from the daisies we'd collected. "Things could have been better, and there were too many hardships to count. I felt like I was always fighting a new battle I couldn't win."

Cora's frail body might have gotten the best of her, but her wise words got the best of me. Death solidifies our purpose here on earth and leaves our legacy behind. Whether it's up a hill or down winding roads, we will end up seeing death as a rite of passage to a better paradise. Perhaps the most honest we will ever be is at the time of our death when we can't outrun ourselves any longer.

• • •

It was 1987, two years after Craig's death. Cora became violently ill. I could no longer care for her when the infection turned to gangrene. She was fighting for her life. Standing in her hospital room, I could hear the pressure from the tubes like a drum vibrating her insides. But nothing ever fooled me with my mother—she'd fight until the very end, battling on death's inescapable playground.

Cora was still there alright, somewhere between heaven and earth, as I watched her eyes twitch to her own screenplay.

I remained at her side, and Tony would stop in occasionally.

"How're you holding up?" He furrowed his brows as he put his arms around me.

"They don't know how much longer, but you know my mum; she always has the final say." I looked back at her, resisting the reality. "I suppose she's just waiting for me to say goodbye, but I'm not sure I can do it."

Tony softly kissed me on the cheek. "Why don't you come home? You need to get some rest."

"Not now. I'll be home tomorrow," I said, returning to rest at Cora's bedside.

When we were left alone, I revisited my memories and drifted back into my childhood.

I could smell Mum's perfume and hear the record needle on the old vinyl, taking me back in time. The record would spin, and I'd sit and listen to Cora hum as she painted her lips and powdered her nose.

She was beautiful back then but also as cold as ice. The images in my memory were disjointed, like the works of Picasso. Paint spilled over my naked body until I was covered in red. I felt betrayed and used, bitter and alone, but most of all, abandoned by a mother who was supposed to protect me. Her domineering, self-indulgent narcissism gripped me like a snake, devouring me slowly. Although I had forgiven her, the little child in me was still wanting her affections to be more than stone images. The child in me wanted to be held.

That evening I cried myself to sleep, just as I had many times before. But at midnight, someone—or something—woke me. A figure was standing at Cora's hospital door.

It moved slowly until it hovered over her, like an angel of darkness. The light in the room was too dim for me to recognize a face. The figure sunk in closer, sniffing the scent of her hospital gown. Was I dreaming?

Overcome with fright, I couldn't move or make a sound as the entity slowly sang a wretched chorus that I couldn't understand. I pretended to be asleep, not daring to jar its presence.

Desperately wanting to scream, my eyes adjusted, and I gasped to see that it was Nelly B, covered in a dark coat. She had come in undetected, smoldering in her insidious plan to attack my mother.

Her crooked smile looked down at Cora, only inches from kissing her forehead. She seemed to be suctioning her life away. I finally forced myself to move, startling her, but again I pretended to be asleep. Nelly B looked around the vacant room, plotting her exit, before making her way down the nurse's hall.

I held my crucifix close to my chest and said the Our Father.

• • •

The next morning Mum's eyes opened slightly. I held her hands and waited patiently until she spoke.

"Jane, I don't want to die and leave you." Cora looked up at the ceiling, nursing her words carefully.

"Oh, Mum, I know you don't want to leave me," I said, trying to hold myself together. "But I don't want you to suffer anymore." I caressed her tired face as her breathing became more labored.

"Who will watch the sunsets with you when I'm gone?"

"Don't be silly; we will watch them together—you'll watch them from high above, while I sit here, down below." I choked over my tears. "Just promise one thing when you get there—promise you'll tell Craig how much I miss him."

Her face turned somber. She brushed her fingers across my skin one last time as a nod of promise before taking her final breath.

"Oh, God. No. Mum!" I shook her to wake her up.

But her lifeless body didn't budge. Her soul was set free, and the little girl in the room was waiting for her mommy to return. I was five all over again.

The world would never know my Cora the way I did. They'd never understand our relationship or the love and war that stood between us. That was mine to keep and no one's to steal.

After her passing, I didn't return to the hillside as I promised. It was a place too painful to experience again. Even though Dean and Tony watched me walk the hill's perimeter, I never went to the top, the grassy wonderland that held so many memories. There was too much to miss, and it was hard to swallow. I think it's a marvel that I didn't go crazy.

• • •

No one would have believed me—that Nelly was the catalyst to my heartbreak. She was a normal aunt and friend to many, but to me, she was dangerous.

Tony was set on logic. Witchcraft was out of the question in his mind. Many people don't believe in it, and they never will until they encounter it. It's safer to just pretend it never happens and walk away.

So that's what I did to distract my mind. I walked, and with the little eyesight I had left, I learned to time streetlights and dodge oncoming traffic as I carried a ten-pound bag of groceries on each arm. There was no way I was going to depend on anybody to get by, and I never have since. Nelly might have thought she'd crippled me, but my resilience was on fire.

• • •

A few months later, Tony's sister Carmela tragically passed away in her sleep. During the funeral, I never made eye contact with Nelly, although her presence was hard to ignore. It was the last time I ever saw her.

Chapter 25

A WALK IN THE CLOUDS

I gazed at the twirling ballerina in my music box and saw myself twirling to the score. But was she happy on her pointed toes, like I, trying to stand firmly on mine?

My mind was in the clouds, as the passing of Craig crushed my reality and left me stubborn from grief.

Tony was the only one who kept me alive through my inner chaos. But when he suffered a massive brain stroke in October 1993, it capsized me.

Dean was in school the afternoon Tony collapsed in our upstairs bedroom. The enormous force of his body hitting the floor startled me and knocked the music box right out of my hands, dislodging the tiny dancer from her platform. I rushed upstairs to find Tony unconscious.

"Tony!" I screamed. "Can you hear me?" But there was no response.

Racing to the telephone, I could barely dial the numbers. "Please! I need an ambulance! My husband is on the floor. He's collapsed and not breathing!" I yelled into the phone, struggling to catch my breath.

Within minutes, the ambulance arrived, lifting Tony onto the stretcher. Dean rushed home from school, then we made our way to the hospital.

I felt my heart skip a beat as we approached Tony's bedside.

"Are you Mrs. Corsaro?" a deep voice from behind me questioned.

"Yes, I'm Mrs. Corsaro." I stepped forward to exit the room, leaving Dean to stay with his father.

"Your husband had a stroke, and there's some internal bleeding," he said, scanning his notes.

"All I care about right now is if he's going to be all right. He's going to be all right, isn't he?" I bargained with the doctor as I looked back at Dean.

"Mrs. Corsaro, all we can do is monitor his progress and stop the bleeding. He'll be here for a few more weeks. We'll run some more tests. I assure you, if we have any more news, we'll let you know."

"I see. Thank you."

After I returned to Tony's bedside, Dean stood up, eager for an update. "So, what did the doctor say?"

I felt my body tremble, but I chose denial to escape the indescribable pain of losing my husband and father to my children.

"They're going to do everything they can, Dean. I promise." I looked down at Tony's unresponsiveness.

"Promise? That's all you do is promise. You promised things would get better after Craig's death—look at us now!" His anger turned into a war against me.

"No, Dean. I didn't promise things would ever get better, but I tried to make it better for all of us. I can't control everything or every outcome or every goddamn thing that happens in our lives!"

Dean became silent. And I found it hard to admit that my family was being torn apart at the seams. Nelly's destructive habits were a menagerie of events, always leading us into her web, even in her absence.

"Your father needs us to be strong, Dean. That's all we can do right now," I said, holding Tony's hand.

• • •

Dean and I watched Tony's slow recovery over the weeks that followed. And in the final week, the doctor gave his instructions.

"He'll be discharged soon. But, Jane, I need you to understand that your husband will never be the same person he was before the stroke. He'll need around-the-clock care, and if it becomes too much for you—"

I stopped him from saying any more. "I understand what you're telling me." I nodded, braving my decision. "When can he come home?"

His weary look said it all, but I pushed the fear behind me.

"He can go home tomorrow. I'll plan to have him transported in the morning. I wish you and your family the best." He said, leaving me to review the paperwork.

The next day couldn't have come sooner. I jumped to my feet as soon as I heard the knock at the door, and I squeezed Tony in my arms like the warrior he was, kissing his mouth repeatedly. He was my hero, and I wished I had said it more throughout all the highs and lows of our marriage. Looking deep into his brown eyes, I could tell how grateful he was to be home.

It was apparent, though, how sensitive his body had become once the transport medic positioned him in our living room chair. Tony moaned from the discomfort. He was an outline of himself, gaunt and drained from the IVs and medications bleeding him dry of nutrients. Though he was barely able to lift a finger, he was brave in heart and sound in mind, determined to win the battle ahead. It was a battle that drove me mad. There were thousands of dollars in hospital bills that helped save his life but left us with crushing debt.

The day he came home, the discharge orders were placed on the front table as if he were a furniture delivery. I wasn't left with a rulebook or a guide for healing wounds. Instead, I was handed a list of numbers and referral resources to help my husband, an incapacitated human whose world had changed overnight.

To keep my husband alive, I had to learn everything I could to properly care for him. That would include speech therapy, rehabilitation, administering his long list of medications, feeding, bathing, and toileting him, among many other tasks.

In his absence, I was a broken woman.

"Love you," Tony struggled to say, looking into my eyes.

"I love you too. Don't worry, honey. We'll get through this. Remember? You always used to tell me that." I nuzzled him, seeing the tears in his eyes build from his strong will.

We navigated the unimaginable and tried to preserve his dignity as I used a washcloth to run warm water down his skin when I bathed him. He was a grown man in a childlike state, dependent on me for everything, but I still had to remain connected to our intimacy. Tony never complained although I'd struggle to lift him in and out of his chair and onto our bed. But when he lay next to me, all appeared normal, as it was before. I'd lean over and kiss him, feeling the tenderness of his lips kiss me back, returning me to womanhood.

"I love you so much," Tony said, trying to reach out and touch me. As difficult as it was for him to show vulnerability, he surrendered.

"Hey, don't do that. Look at me! We'll get through this, won't we?" My heart began to feel like it was dying with him. "There's nothing we can't do, Tony. You taught me that. Every time I wanted to hide or give up, you opened the curtains to show me the light. That was you!" I encouraged him while holding his face in my hands.

Tony spoke with power and passion. "I opened the curtains so you wouldn't be afraid anymore of what you couldn't see. I didn't want you to suffer or feel pain, Jane." His eyes grew tired.

"Try to get some rest," I said. I lay my head against the pillow. "You saved me, Tony. Always remember that." And he did. He was everything to me that had seemed impossible to come true.

• • •

Over the many years that followed, we kept each other strong. And when Dean was home from college, he and Tony would spend hours together, sitting on the porch, watching the rain fall or the leaves tumble away. The two men admired and respected each other—there was no one closer to Dean than his father.

Tony's strength never fully returned, but his speech improved little by little. In the days of our trials and tribulations, a part of me felt like I was walking in the clouds, separated from reality but clinging to a dream.

However, my life was just a story I had to grow from. Though my progressive blindness had hindered me for years, I didn't let it hold me back. Walking home from the grocery store, the sounds of the cars were intimidating, but the night never scared me. The little girl from McKeesport was already familiar with the blind alleys.

"I'm home!" I shouted to Tony, who was sitting in the living room watching television.

"There's my girl," he said, motioning his arms for me to come closer.

I hugged him tightly, leaving a red patch of lipstick on the side of his cheek. "I'm making a roast tonight—your favorite!" I headed to grab the pots and pans for supper.

"Let me help you," Tony insisted, trying to force himself off the recliner.

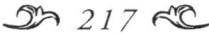

"No, I've got it. Don't you be stubborn!" I yelled back from the kitchen, looking around the corner to make sure he was still sitting upright.

"For heaven's sake, just let me help you!" His voice became louder and more agitated, right before he lost his balance and collapsed on the floor.

"Tony! Why don't you ever listen to me?"

"I can do it, goddamn it!" he screamed over the television, pushing my arms away. "I'm a man, aren't I? I'm not some fucking imbecile!" He tried to push himself up. "I used to do everything for everyone around here—fix the car, the roof, and now what do I do? I sit here and watch television all day while you cook and clean!"

It took me a few tries lifting him, but eventually, he was back in his recliner. However, Tony's unhappiness weighed more heavily on my mind than the weight of his body. After supper, I wiped the sides of his face and washed the last bit of dishes. Then the telephone rang.

"Hello, Jane. It's Nelly B. I heard about Tony. I'll be in the area next week and wanted to see about taking the two of you for a trip to Niagara Falls. It's beautiful up there, and you'd be close enough to catch the view."

"Your timing is impeccable, Nelly," I said, after taking a deep breath to calm my nerves. In the back of my mind, I could only imagine her horrendous plan to drive us off the cliff.

"Nelly, he isn't in any shape to go on a trip, let alone Niagara Falls."

I could hear Nelly sigh with disappointment.

"You know, if I didn't like you, I would've run you both off the cliff." She laughed, confirming my suspicions. "OK, then. Well, if you change your mind, you know where to reach me." She sounded as if we'd missed a great opportunity.

Despite all her nasty attempts, Nelly eventually moved to Texas. And every now and again, she'd send us a postcard with these words:

"Don't mess with Texas!" Probably as a threat. But as the cards arrived, I'd shred them and toss them in the trash.

I was no longer afraid of her.

As I ran my fingers through Tony's hair, I watched the night's clouds rock us both to sleep. But night was designed for curiosity. The more I looked at it, the more the blackness became beautiful and mysterious, like our lives. Somewhere between here and eternity, we are floating among the stars, wrestling with our fates and never being promised a new day. But what was promised was right now, here in our space, with Tony's head resting next to mine.

Chapter 26

BABY BLUES

"With every new generation, things transition. I know it's inevitable, but they say if it's not broken, don't fix it. I must come from a radical time, from another planet, because in today's age, I wonder if we've lost our marbles. When I was younger, we believed in marriage and family. It was our core roots in faith that raised our children to continue building community, not abandoning it. We had values and morals. But now, the generations have changed; the family dynamic has fallen apart, somewhere between social media and a smoke shop. I saw it happen slowly, and the more independent-minded we became from our roots, the more we tolerated the new divide. We didn't know ourselves anymore. We always wanted more, but we didn't know why. We were lost without direction and without our faith to keep us together."

—JANE CORSARO

"Hi, Mom. I'm going to have a baby," Dean said over the phone, catching me off guard.

"With who? Wait, hold on for a second, your father wants to know what's happening." I turned to yell around the corner. "Our son is going to have a baby!"

"A what?" Tony shouted.

"A baby!"

"A puppy?" Tony struggled to hear.

"Never mind. I'll tell you later!" I said, resting my vocal cords and turning back to Dean. "Who is she?"

"A girl I've been dating for a while. Anyway, Mom, she's eight months pregnant. I'm sorry I haven't told you guys, but I've been working a lot and trying to plan. It's been pretty difficult."

"Well, I'm sure, honey … but when will we meet her?" I asked while casually peeling potatoes.

"We're going through a lot right now. Maybe eventually. We'll see how things work out." Dean ended the conversation.

• • •

Before we knew it, our grandson was born—and it was the first time I'd met Ashley. She looked like a child herself, barely pushing eighteen and carefree in nature.

"He's beautiful!" I said, cradling his tiny body.

"Hello, baby. Hello, my little angel." I spoke tenderly, kissing his forehead, reimagining the first time I held my two boys in my arms.

Ashley and Dean went their separate ways shortly after his birth, but who could blame them? They were just kids themselves.

• • •

A few months later, Dean arrived at my doorstep.

"Mom, I need your help. Could you watch DJ for a while, just until I get everything under control?" He looked down at his watch.

"What's the matter, Dean?" I asked, careful not to intervene in his affairs.

"I can't explain everything right now. I'm just asking for this one favor. Will you do it?"

"Of course, I'll help you. I'm his grandmother, aren't I? But I need to discuss this with your father," I said, looking over at Tony, who had just been regaining his strength.

"Thank you, Mom." Dean swung DJ's things over my shoulder and bundled him from the cold.

Back inside, I rehearsed what I'd tell Tony before waking him with a newborn in my arms.

"Dean needs us to watch DJ for a while," I said, turning off the nightly news.

"For how long?" Tony's eyes opened just enough to show he was coherent.

DJ hiccupped and drooled over the bath towel, fussing for Tony's attention.

"I don't know. Just for a while, I guess."

"Well, what's the matter with him—can't he get a job?" Tony rose, looking for the time. "Tell our son he needs to get things figured out." He rubbed the sleep from his eyes and looked at me sternly. "Honey, listen. How are you going to take care of both of us, let alone an infant?"

Tony had a point, and I knew it, though I couldn't resist DJ's toothless grin as he stared at us, innocently entertained.

After settling DJ down in his highchair, I searched for the right words to convince Tony further.

"I feel in debt to Dean," I admitted, not realizing I was scooping mounds of vegetables onto Tony's plate.

"Well, if you insist you can do it, then OK." Tony paused, kissing DJ and tickling his sides.

The next morning, I received another phone call from Dean.

"Please, Mom, you've got to watch him through the end of the year. I've just been offered a great opportunity that I can't afford to lose!"

Somewhere between mixing baby formula and watching the burner cook our stew, I gave my blessing.

"Just promise me you're all right."

"I am. Thanks, Mom. I'll call you soon."

• • •

There were many sleepless nights, bottle feedings, playtimes, and temper tantrums. I became a mother all over again, and our grandson's energy was just like his father's. He'd scoot around the house, mesmerized by everything he could get his sticky fingers on.

"Would you tell him to quiet down? I'm trying to hear the weather report!" Tony yelled from his chair.

"Hold on a sec! I'm about to burn the meatloaf!"

"I can't hear! They're saying something about a storm coming in, and I've got this little weasel using his windpipes like he's Eddie Fisher."

"Just a minute! For heaven's sake, Tony, he's just a little boy—not a windup toy!" I said, carrying DJ to his highchair.

• • •

Eventually, Tony learned to control his temper, and the two of them found a happy medium. Whether it was playing hide-and-seek or building blocks, DJ loved his grandfather's attention, so much so that Tony became humored by it. They'd spend hours together playing train station while Tony tooted the horn and made engine sounds that delighted DJ's imagination. They were inseparable.

My grandson was undoubtedly loved, but he grew homesick for his parents. Whenever DJ had the chance to visit with his father, he'd follow him everywhere, admiring his every word and showering him with affection. But when Dean left, we filled in the missing pieces.

• • •

A new year had arrived, and it was time to sing Happy Birthday. DJ took a deep breath to blow out his candles and told us he wanted to become a superhero when he grew up.

"Make a wish, sweetie, and it will come true," I said, holding him over the tiny flame.

"OK, Grandma. I've got a good one this year!" He puckered his lips.

Suddenly, there was a knock at the front door.

"Who could that be?" I said, glancing over my shoulder.

"Go ahead and cut the cake, honey. I'll be right back," I said, untying my apron.

I was greeted by the mailman, shivering in the unforgiving wind.

"Have a nice day, miss." He bowed his head politely, handing over a white envelope.

Carefully, not to tear the inside, I opened it.

April 15, 1995
"It is with great sorrow, I write to tell you that
my mother, Nelly B, has passed away."
Sincerely,
Leonard

"Oh my God," I gasped.

My hands lost grip of the letter, causing it to fall like a delicate feather from my fingertips to the floor below. It was a shock and my mind transported me back to Nelly's lair, where I kneeled before her sorcery. It was like a death sentence had been lifted. I rejoiced. Outside, the wind gusts stirred, and I knew it had all ended. She couldn't hurt us anymore.

After her death, I mourned, even though it seemed odd to do so. I didn't understand her malevolence, but I understood her pain. I'll remember her in every Pennsylvania dark sky, in the embers of Brick Alley, and in every jealous face. The wicked may never heal, but we can empathize with them. She would have murdered all of us, I believe. One by one, we would have psychologically or physically paid the price. But now she was laid to rest—or perhaps she was awaiting judgment.

> *"Here and now, all is still, in our little red house*
> *on the hill. Where the shadows drift far apart,*
> *no one speaks of her black heart.*
> *Goodnight, Nelly B. Good Night."*
>
> —JANE CORSARO

Chapter 27

CHARIOT OF TRUTH

"I've held onto this story for so many years,
but now it's time to put it to rest."

—JANE CORSARO

After Tony had his second stroke, I was in debt. The medical system had taken most of our life savings.

For many years, night after night and day after day, I fought resiliently to survive the ambush of one medical bill after the other. In addition to hospital bills, there were medication costs and expensive therapies to keep my husband stable.

I felt like I was an underground drug lord, inviting unwanted guests in and out of my home so they could push experimental pharmaceuticals down his throat. But I didn't have a choice because, without them, he would have died.

When help was unavailable, Tony would lie in his own feces until someone arrived. So, I became his 24/7 nurse. There were no breaks. I tried to keep him clean, but the stench permeated our home, spilling from the underpad onto the floor, making its way into places all over his body that I'd discover while cleaning him up. The smell would have made most people gag and vomit, but I didn't have time to focus on anything else but his withering body.

That's when God would step in. We don't have the power to do it alone nor take on a crisis by ourselves. Whatever trauma a person endures, they'll receive an awakening from a divine source, a source they can't always describe, but it will always be present in times of need.

You can't always call a loved one or a friend. Sometimes all you can do is pray. So that's what I did. I spoke to God on the long walks home. I asked him many things, but most of all, I asked him to save my Tony. It was a chariot of truth that was at my doorstep. I couldn't be absorbed in tomorrow. I could only live for today.

• • •

Tony was rushed to the hospital after suffering another series of strokes many years later. With a severe thunderstorm forming, I remained home while Dean rushed to the hospital.

My son called to tell me the news.

Tony was pronounced deceased before they could operate.

"Goodbye, my darling," I whispered, as the rain trickled down the windowpane, and I watched the lightning light up the room.

But I wasn't really alone. Tony's spiritual presence came upon me. My darling was finally at peace.

He passed away in September 2014.

• • •

The next afternoon, a large procession of neighbors passed in front of our house. The sky was cloudless and resurrected from the prior night's rains. Friends young and old came to pay their respects and lay flowers over my fence.

The young child in me returned once again. I pressed my hands on the windowsill, peering out into a world that was changing by the minute. Life will overtly have us rise and fall again and again. It's the chariot of truth. But we can survive tragedy and breath once more after the storms pass.

Chapter 28

Beyond the Sunset

Four years later

"Jane! Jane, are you in there?" My neighbor Harry tapped at the screen, looking for signs of life.

I opened the door, fatigued and squinting at the light outside that hurt my eyes.

"I came to check on you. Are you all right?" he asked. "I'm headed to the store and was going to pick you up a few things."

Harry's body looked morbidly feeble. He was barely able to hold himself up on his ancient cane.

"Could you pick me up a pack of Bud Light?" I shamefully asked, rubbing my eyes to adjust to the sun.

"Now, Jane, you know better than that. Mabel would kill me if she found out I was buying you booze. I'll be back with some soup and crackers." He bid me farewell as his ninety-year-old frame inched down the walkway.

"OK," I said with a shrug before retiring to the couch.

My body was tired. I opened a pack of chips and munched, enjoying the salty serenity. I was in my eighties and weighed only ninety pounds after living off baked beans, chips, and Cheerios for months.

Shortly after Tony's death, Dean and DJ moved to Las Vegas where Dean married and made a life for himself far from the trials of this small town.

The only hero I had left was my neighbor Harry. He'd help me write my checks to cover the past-due balances and late fees that had piled up.

I survived by the skin of my teeth. Had it not been for my pension and the railroad checks from Tony's retirement, I'd have been homeless. It was a cruel world, and it was still unforgiving.

My town's sidewalks were empty. No sounds. Parks were empty, and the train tracks were abandoned. Even the local businesses were graffitied and boarded shut. The lifeblood was dry, bone dry from the gluttony and sewage spilling from men's fingertips. You could smell it on every corner as it eroded the rooftops.

"Am I dead?" I asked my alter ego while savoring the last crunch in my mouth and listening to the silence engulf me.

"Nope, I can still hear those damn pigeons!" I laughed, shooing them off the glass frame.

When Tony passed, our home deteriorated. The rooftop needed work, the grass was overgrown, and the cobwebs were forming a fiesta in my parlor. I was being buried alive, just like Mum, but in the comforts of my own home. It's a place we'd all rather be before retiring to dust. I was en route, or at least it felt like it.

• • •

When I learned Harry had died, the layers of my life peeled away. I spent hours lying in the abyss, hours listening to the vibrations of the universe sift through my veins. I realized it was the pits of hell that made me the greatest actress I'd ever know—and God, who kept me standing on my feet, that made me a believer.

I'd walked the darkest streets, ran from the wolves, carried my crosses, and buried my losses. I don't think there will be closure, but I think a spiritual awakening takes place when you realize you're a survivor.

I've repented a thousand times to God, slain the devil in his wicked stare, and trumped the deck of cards I was given. All to find grace. Standing in my wizardry, I found peace.

The messages I received just before Craig's passing inspired me to tell my story. They were messages from God. People would often ask me how I know God is real. And I'd tell them this: God inspired the wise men, and we are no different. His timing is perfect. If only human beings would understand that they don't need to solve every riddle life offers. The magic will offer itself at the time of death when we can see it more clearly. Until then, we stubbornly see, hear, and feel only what we want to—rather than believe with the incarnate force of faith.

Back in the Glory Room, a caregiver asked what lighting a candle meant to me, and I told her, "If we carry our burdens with dignity and grace and be kind to others, at the end of life's journey, no matter who we are or where we are, rich or poor, the golden light of Jesus Christ will shine upon us. That's what it means to me. And when I transition from this life, and my body is no more, I know I'll be reunited with those I've loved until the ends of eternity, and I'll run so fast I'll break away from these earthly chains into a paradise that lives in my dreams."

I'm ready to give my chair to another person now. This little girl has grown up and is too wise for her britches. I just pray that God takes me peacefully in my sleep. It was a beautiful story … it was my life.

Epilogue

FROM THE AUTHOR

"You'll use your talents to paint the hearts of the world, Samantha, when I'm gone. And one day, when time passes, remember how thankful I was for your friendship. Remember … human hearts forever intertwine, somewhere in time, somewhere beyond the sunset."

— JANE CORSARO

March 2020. A deadly pandemic spread rapidly over the world. It turned our lives upside down and tore apart our homes and communities. We were blindsided.

My hands were sore from writing, but my head was full of worry—I knew I must keep going. Inside, I could feel the uncertainty build; the lack of normalcy choked me in my sleep. I had nightmares. I couldn't escape the turmoil and the fear of infection.

After I returned to work on the front lines, I knew I shared a pivotal role in the lives of those in the Glory Room. I knew I had to keep them motivated, especially during our darkest days. Not only did the pandemic separate us from each other, but the isolation from the outside world was just as bad, and some of our residents would lose their will to live. I was scared not only of risking my own health but of failing them, and I wasn't able to get to everyone. How do you choose between yourself and the lives of the most vulnerable when you head into a war zone you know nothing about?

By mid-March, the Glory Room shifted to lockdown. Signs were placed in our front windows prohibiting anyone from the outside—other than medical professionals—from accessing our facility. Family members couldn't enter. They could only visit from the outside, viewing through the windows.

Our hearts were shattered, but we remained resilient. One day, I found Jane walking up and down the hallways, hurrying to her own tune. She had just come back from her hometown and was wearing a mask and gloves. She was excited to see me and hurried me back to her apartment to review the cases of pictures I'd asked her to bring back from McKeesport. After all these years, the photos had tattered edges but were mainly intact.

I entered her quaint space, expecting a photo reunion with the characters I'd imagined in her story. Instantly, I was overcome by an aromatic scent of freshly brewed coffee and the Covid death-toll numbers blaring from her television. Jane turned it down, then nursed her cup of coffee and settled beside the pictures spread across her comforter. She appeared poised and unaltered by the news.

The first portrait left me speechless. Cora and Martin peered back at me with telling eyes, while Jane pointed to herself standing between her two parents as a young child. She introduced them to me as if they were standing there, still living. But there was one photograph that particularly haunted me—a picture of Jane and her family sitting around the dining room table, stuck in the remnants of time, unaware of the future. They smiled candidly, showcasing their personalities on the surface, but beneath it all, there was something hidden.

Next, she handed me a picture of Craig. His intense eyes appeared to look back at me as if troubled by something.

I cupped her life story in my hands as it cascaded like rippling waves over an embankment. Each picture revealed a story, a secret. So now, even after death, Jane's loved ones appear vividly in my imagination.

"Wasn't he handsome?" Jane teared up, touching the faded Polaroid print of Craig's face before kissing it. "He'd just turned seventeen in that photo."

I sat beside her. Although protocol tells us to keep our distance, we hugged, and she began to sob.

Those were strange times when we couldn't decipher emotion behind our masks or allow human contact within six feet. Jane leaned over my shoulder, burying her sorrow into the lining of my sweater, then quickly collected herself and grabbed a tissue.

"We'll catch up soon, Jane." I smiled before walking out, leaving her door slightly ajar.

Back at home, I felt a sense of accomplishment. I'd gathered my clues to Jane's story, resurrecting the pieces I needed to understand each person's contribution to her life. She'd unknowingly challenged me throughout this process and made me more aware of my purpose.

Life is a precious gift. If I'm a believer that we exist after death, then our souls move onward after we're no longer housed in our bodies. The beauty of this journey is seeing our brokenness rebirthed by a merciful God. He provides each of us an opportunity to overcome every obstacle. And, in return for overcoming our obstacles, he shows us a better reflection of ourselves.

There is a place and time for everything. Jane and I were destined to meet and journey together to write her story.

May we all live peacefully beyond the sunset, my dear Jane. And may we not forget that the Glory Room shines and celebrates each soul that passes through. I'll carry the torch of your story in my heart forever to help me tell other people's stories with the love I've told yours.

About Samantha Noelle

Samantha currently resides in Sedona, Arizona. Even as a young child, she felt the desire to help others. Whether it was volunteering at senior centers or finding someone who needed an ear to listen, she always felt she was a light worker at heart, here to help others heal and live their best life.

That calling led to a fulfilling career as an Activity Director for senior living centers in both Nevada and Arizona, where she restructured and developed engaging programs to help promote healthy aging.

Samantha also enjoys being a creative intuitive. Whether it's songwriting or practicing reiki healing, she focuses her talents on the arts to inspire and uplift the lives of many.

She's always been driven by compassion and a heart that never stops giving. Recently, she felt called to venture to Sedona, Arizona to continue her mission work where she helps people from all around the world find their spirituality.

Samantha desires to continue telling people's stories—as she did Jane's—to enlighten the world and let others know that there is purpose to all our lives. We need to use our gifts and keep on giving.

Contact the Author

Samantha Noelle may be contacted via her email:
beyondborderspublishing@gmail.com

Visit her website:
www.beyondborderspublishing.com